Nelson Thornes **Framework English**

Access
Skills in **Fiction**

Wendy Wren

Series Consultant: **John Jackman**
Scottish Consultant: **Sandra Ferguson**

Contents

Section	Text type	Word	Sentence	Writing	Page
Unit 1 There are more things in heaven and earth					
1 *Johnny and the Dead* Terry Pratchett	Modern fiction	Vocabulary: dictionary and contextual work Spelling: derivations	Nouns and adjectives	Descriptive writing	4
2 *Dracula* Bram Stoker, adapted by Jim Alderson	Classic fiction	Vocabulary: dictionary and contextual work Spelling: syllables	Prepositions	Descriptive writing	10
3 *Gabriel-Ernest* Saki (H H Munro)	Short story	Vocabulary: dictionary and contextual work Spelling: vowel sounds ie/ei	Conjunctions	Descriptive writing	16
Unit 2 I have a dream					
1 *The Goalkeeper's Revenge* Bill Naughton	Short story	Vocabulary: dictionary and contextual work Spelling: common prefixes	Sentence types	Story openings Third person	22
2 *Rebecca* Daphne du Maurier	Classic fiction	Vocabulary: dictionary and contextual work Spelling: prefixes making antonyms	Subject and verb	Story openings First person	28
3 *Metamorphosis* Franz Kafka	Modern fiction	Vocabulary: dictionary and contextual work Spelling: prefixes	Subject and predicate	Story openings	34
Unit 3 As one great furnace flamed					
1 *The Bed and Breakfast Star* Jacqueline Wilson	Modern fiction	Vocabulary: dictionary and contextual work Spelling: suffixes ing/ed	Simple and compound sentences	Crises in stories First person	40
2 *The Firework Display* George Layton	Short story	Vocabulary: dictionary and contextual work Spelling: common homophones	Complex sentences	Crises in stories	46
3 *Lord of the Flies* William Golding	Modern classic	Vocabulary: dictionary and contextual work Spelling: soft and hard c	Adjectival clauses	Complications in stories	52

Section	Text type	Word	Sentence	Writing	Page
Unit 4 Red in tooth and claw					
1 *Reynard the Fox* John Masefield	Narrative poetry	Vocabulary: dictionary and contextual work Spelling: suffix ion	Adjectival clauses	Narrative poetry	58
2 *Owls* Leonard Clark	Descriptive poetry	Vocabulary: dictionary and contextual work Spelling: plurals s/es	Noun and verb	Descriptive poetry	64
3 *My Mother Saw a Dancing Bear* Charles Causley	Narrative poetry	Vocabulary: dictionary and contextual work Spelling: unstressed vowels	Punctuating poetry	Narrative poetry	70
Unit 5 Let slip the dogs of war					
1 *War Game* Michael Foreman	Modern fiction	Vocabulary: dictionary and contextual work Spelling: plurals – words ending in y	Powerful verbs	Story endings – cliff-hangers	76
2 *Mission Control: Hannibal One* Len Deighton	Modern short story	Vocabulary: dictionary and contextual work Spelling: suffixes ous/ious	Direct speech	Story endings – unexpected	82
3 *Space Weed* David Orme	Modern fiction	Vocabulary: dictionary and contextual work Spelling: suffixes able/ible	Conditional sentences	Story endings – building tension	88
Unit 6 All the world's a stage					
1 *Animal Rights* Michael Church and Betty Tadman	Modern play	Vocabulary: dictionary and contextual work Spelling: suffix ful	Active and passive verbs	Playscripts	94
2 *Kidsplay* John Lee	Modern play	Vocabulary: dictionary and contextual work Spelling: contractions and 'not' words	Punctuating a playscript	Dramatic dialogue	100
3 *Bugsy Malone* Alan Parker	Film script	Vocabulary: dictionary and contextual work Spelling: apostrophe of possession – singular	Standard and non-Standard English	Storyboards	106

Unit 1 There are more things in heaven and earth / fiction

There was the Alderman...

The story so far... Johnny has seen dead people in the cemetery. His friends, Wobbler, Yo-less and Bigmac think he is pulling their legs. Johnny takes them there to prove he is telling the truth but he is the only one who can see the dead...

There was the Alderman, and William Stickers, and an old woman in a long dress and a hat covered in fruit, and some small children running on ahead, and dozens, *hundreds* of others. They didn't lurch. They didn't ooze green. They just looked grey and very slightly out of focus.

You notice things when you're terrified. Little details grow bigger.

He realised there were differences among the dead. Mr Vicenti had looked almost... well, alive. William Stickers was slightly more colourless. The Alderman was definitely transparent around the edges. But many of the others, in Victorian clothes and odd assortments of coats and breeches from earlier ages, were almost completely without colour and

Johnny and the Dead

Extract / **1.1**

almost without <u>substance</u>, so that they were little more than shaped air, but air that walked.

It wasn't that they had faded. It was just that they were further away, in some strange direction that had nothing much to do with the normal three.

Wobbler and the other two were still staring at him.

'Johnny? You all right?' said Wobbler.

Johnny remembered a piece about over population in a school Geography book. For everyone who was alive today, it said, there were twenty historical people, all the way back to when people had only just *become* people.

Or, to put it another way, behind every living person were twenty dead ones.

Quite a lot of them were behind Wobbler. Johnny didn't feel it would be a good idea to point this out, though.

'It's gone all cold,' said Bigmac.

'We ought to be getting back,' said Wobbler, his voice shaking. 'I ought to be doing my homework.'

Which showed he *was* frightened. It'd take <u>zombies</u> to make Wobbler prefer to do his homework.

'You can't see them, can you,' said Johnny. 'They're all around us, but you can't see them.'

'The living can't generally see the dead,' said Mr Vicenti. 'It's for their own good, I expect.'

The three boys had drawn closer together.

'Come on, stop mucking about,' said Bigmac.

'Huh,' said Wobbler. 'He's just trying to spook us. Huh. Like Dead Man's Hand at parties. Huh. Well, it's not working. I'm off home. Come on, you lot.'

He turned and walked a few steps.

'Hang on,' said Yo-less. 'There's something odd –'

He looked around at the empty cemetery. The rook had flown away, unless it was a crow.

'Something odd,' he mumbled.

'Look,' said Johnny. 'They're here! They're all around us!'

Terry Pratchett

COMPREHENSION

A Copy these sentences. Fill in the missing words.

1 The old woman wore a _ _ _ _ dress and a hat covered in _ _ _ _ _.

2 The Alderman was _ _ _ _ _ _ _ _ _ _ _ around the edges.

3 Johnny didn't feel it was a good _ _ _ _ to tell Wobbler what was behind him.

4 Wobbler wanted to go and do his _ _ _ _ _ _ _.

5 Wobbler thought that Johnny was just trying to _ _ _ _ _ his friends.

Unit 1 There are more things in heaven and earth / fiction

B 1 Three of the 'dead' people are named. What are their names?

2 What does Johnny notice about the dead people *'from earlier ages'*?

3 What does Johnny soon realise about his friends?

4 Yo-less thinks that there is *'something odd'*. What two things do the boys notice that are unusual?

5 Why do you think that Mr Vicenti says that it is *'for their own good'* that the living cannot generally see the dead?

C Explain in your own words how the four boys reacted to the situation.

VOCABULARY

Use a dictionary and the context of the story to explain the following words. They are underlined in the passage. The first one is done for you.

1 Alderman = member of the local council   2 lurch   3 ooze

4 focus   5 substance   6 zombies

SPELLING

The English language we speak today is made up of many words which have come from other languages. We have been invaded by the Romans, German tribes, and the French and many of their words, in some form, are part of our language today.

The words in the box come from the extract you have read. Copy them and match them with the words in the table.

HINT

Many of the words look similar.

dozen   home   air   idea   living

Word	Language	Meaning
aira	Old French	atmosphere
lifde	Old English	to have life
dozeine	Old French	twelve
ham	Old English	dwellings
idealis	Latin	mental image

Johnny and the Dead

Activity / **1.1**

GRAMMAR AND PUNCTUATION

Nouns and adjectives

> **Nouns** are naming words.
>
> **Common nouns** are the names of things which you can see and touch.
> eg *the hat   the book   the crow*
>
> **Proper nouns** are the names of people and places. They begin with a capital letter.
> eg *William Stickers   Wobbler*
>
> **Collective nouns** are the names of groups of things.
> eg *the people*
>
> **Abstract nouns** are the names of qualities, feelings and times. You cannot see or touch them.
> eg *the idea   the cold*

A Copy the table and use a tick to show which type of noun each word is.

noun	common	proper	collective	abstract
Mr Vicenti				
homework				
fear				
zombies				
crowd				
Bigmac				
bravery				

B Choose three of the nouns in the table and write a sentence using each one.

> **Adjectives** are describing words. They tell us more about a noun, eg its colour, size, smell, taste, sound, etc.

C What nouns in the extract are these adjectives describing? The first one is done for you.

1 colourless = William Stickers
2 transparent
3 shaped
4 strange
5 historical
6 empty

Unit 1 There are more things in heaven and earth / fiction

Johnny and the Dead

Activity / **1.1**

WRITING

Writing descriptions

> Descriptive writing helps the reader to see what is being written about.
>
> Good descriptive writing paints a picture with words.

Language features

Adjectives

Adjectives help a reader to imagine what things:

- look like (sight)
- feel like (touch)
- taste like
- sound like
- smell like.

Copy the phrases and write to which sense the adjective is appealing. The first one is done for you.

1. beautiful dress = *sight*
2. spicy meal
3. stale odour
4. tuneless singing
5. smooth surface
6. empty cemetery

Precise choice of words

Some adjectives have been used so much they are boring! You need to think of really interesting adjectives for your descriptions.

eg *Johnny isn't just frightened, he is 'terrified'.*

William Stickers is not just a bit dull, he is 'slightly more colourless'.

Replace these boring adjectives with interesting ones.

1. a *cold* night
2. an *old* headstone
3. a *nice* hat
4. a *big* crow
5. a *small* boy
6. a *good* book

Writing assignment

In the extract, the author tells us that there are 'hundreds' of other ghosts in the cemetery.

Think carefully about what one of these ghosts might look like.

Write a description of the ghost.

Remember to use interesting adjectives so your reader can really see the ghost.

Paint a picture with words!

Unit 1 There are more things in heaven and earth / fiction

I heard a heavy step...

Jonathan Harker is a young lawyer. He makes a long journey to Count Dracula to advise him about buying a house in London. He arrives after midnight at Dracula's castle.

I heard a heavy step behind the great door. I looked through a <u>chink</u> and saw a light coming towards me. There was the sound of rattling chains. I heard the clanking of huge bolts being drawn back. A key turned with a loud scraping noise. The great door swung back.

Dracula

Extract / **1.2**

A tall old man stood there. He was <u>clean-shaven</u> except for a long white moustache. He was dressed in black from head to foot and held an old silver lamp. This lamp sent long shadows over the door. The old man spoke very good English but his voice sounded rather odd.

'Welcome to my house. <u>Enter</u> of your own free will.'

As soon as I went through the doorway, he rushed forward. He grabbed my hand. The power of his grip made me <u>gasp</u> with pain. His hand felt as cold as ice. It was more like the hand of a dead man than a living man.

'Count Dracula?' I asked.

He bowed. 'Yes. I am Dracula,' he replied. 'You are welcome to my house, Mr Harker. Come in. The night air is cold, and you need to eat and rest.'

He picked up my bags and led me to a room. It was well lit. A table was laid for supper and some logs burned brightly in the fire. Then he showed me my bedroom. I had a wash and went down for supper.

'Please sit down and eat,' he said. 'I have already eaten and I do not drink.'

I handed him a letter from Mr Hawkins, the head of my firm. The Count read the letter. I told him all that had happened on my journey. As I talked, I looked at him more closely. He was an odd man. His face was strong and his eyebrows were very bushy. Under his white moustache, his mouth was <u>cruel</u>. His teeth were very pointed and stuck out over his red lips. His ears were white and pointed at the top. His skin was very, very pale. It was almost <u>bloodless</u>. His hands were thick and powerful. The nails were long and cut to sharp points. And there were hairs growing from the middle of his palms!

The Count leaned over to talk to me. I shivered. His breath was so bad I wanted to be sick all over the carpet. He noticed my shiver. He leaned back with a strange smile. For a while we were both silent. Then, I heard the wolves again. They were in the valley below.

The Count's eyes lit up and he said, 'Listen to them. They are the children of the night. What music they make!'

Then he got up and said, 'But you must be tired. Your bedroom is all ready. You may sleep as long as you wish. I will be away until tomorrow afternoon. Sleep well and have pleasant dreams!'

*Bram Stoker,
adapted by Jim Alderson*

COMPREHENSION

A Write 'true' or 'false' for each of these statements.

1. The door to Count Dracula's house was locked.
2. Count Dracula could not speak very good English.
3. Count Dracula and Mr Harker had supper together.
4. Mr Harker had brought a letter for the Count.
5. They heard dogs barking outside.

Unit 1 There are more things in heaven and earth / fiction

B 1 Find and copy three phrases which describe Count Dracula as he stands in the doorway.

2 Find and copy three of the 'odd' things Mr Harker noticed about the Count.

3 How do you know that Mr Harker arrived at night?

4 Why did Mr Harker want *'to be sick all over the carpet'*?

5 How do you know the Count was pleased to hear the wolves howling?

C Explain in your own words how you think Mr Harker was feeling as he went to his bedroom.

VOCABULARY

Use a dictionary and the context of the passage to explain the meanings of these words. They are underlined in the passage. The first one is done for you.

1 chink = small crack   2 clean-shaven   3 enter

4 gasp   5 cruel   6 bloodless

SPELLING

> **Syllables** are sounds that make up a word.
> Each syllable makes a sound of its own.
> All syllables have a vowel sound.
> *noise* is pronounced   *noise*   It has one syllable.
> *shadow* is pronounced   *sha/dow*   It has two syllables.
> *powerful* is pronounced *pow/er/ful* It has three syllables.

Copy each word and divide it into syllables. Underline the vowel sounds. The first one has been done for you.

1 behind   b<u>e</u>/h<u>i</u>nd
2 rattling
3 key
4 moustache
5 silver
6 Dracula
7 already
8 children

> **HINT**
> *Dividing up words into syllables helps your spelling.*

12

Dracula

Activity / **1.2**

GRAMMAR AND PUNCTUATION

Prepositions are words which tell us where something is.
eg 'I heard a heavy step **behind** the great door.'
'This lamp sent long shadows **over** the door.'

A Write the prepositions in these sentences.
The first one is done for you.

1 I went through the doorway.   through
2 Under his white moustache, his mouth was cruel.
3 Supper was on the table.
4 There were hairs growing from the middle of his palms.
5 Count Dracula was seated at the table.
6 The wolves were in the valley.

B Write the opposites of these prepositions.
The first one is done for you.

1 in   out
2 inside
3 above
4 off
5 up
6 near
7 before
8 over
9 in front of

HINT

Opposites are also known as antonyms.

C The prepositions in bold are not correct. Write the sentences correctly.
The first one is done for you.

1 Mr Harker entered **into** the door.

   Mr Harker entered through the door.

2 Mr Harker knocked **to** the door.
3 Count Dracula went **in** the dining room.
4 Mr Harker was frightened **off** the Count.
5 He had come **for** a long way that night.
6 The wolves were heard **on** the silence.

Unit 1 There are more things in heaven and earth / fiction

Dracula

Activity / **1.2**

WRITING

Writing descriptions

> When you write a **description** of a person you should have a clear picture in your mind of what that person looks like.

Language features

Physical details

Mr Harker's description of Count Dracula is very precise. He considers:

- his size and age
  'A tall old man'
- his facial appearance
  'He was clean-shaven except for a long white moustache.'
  '... his mouth was cruel'
  'His teeth were pointed and stuck out over his red lips.'
  'His ears were white and pointed at the top.'
  'His skin was very, very pale.'
- his voice
  'The old man spoke very good English but his voice sounded rather odd.'
- unusual features
  'The nails were long and cut to sharp points.'
  'And there were hairs growing from the middle of his palms!'
  'His breath was so bad'

Given what you already know about Count Dracula, write a short description of his hair and eyes.

Similes

Some writers use **similes** to make their description more vivid. Similes are phrases using 'like' or 'as' to compare things.

Count Dracula's hands are not just cold. They are 'as cold as ice'.

Write similes to describe Count Dracula's:

- nails
- moustache
- lips.

Writing assignment

Imagine you are Count Dracula. Write a description of Mr Harker as you first see him at the door and look more closely at him over supper.

The picture on the opposite page will help you.

Unit 1 There are more things in heaven and earth / fiction

...this wild-looking boy...

In this story, the character Van Cheele is walking through a wood when he meets a young boy...

Where on earth could this wild-looking boy <u>hail</u> from? The miller's wife had lost a child some two months ago, supposed to have been swept away by the river, but that had been a mere baby, not a half grown lad.

'What are you doing there?' he demanded.
'Obviously, sunning myself.' replied the boy.
'Where do you live?'
'Here, in the woods.'
'You can't live in the woods,' said Van Cheele.
'They are very nice woods,' said the boy.

Gabriel-Ernest

Extract / 1.3

'But where do you sleep at night?'

'I don't sleep at night; that's my busiest time.'

Van Cheele began to have an <u>irritated</u> feeling that the boy was trying to make a fool of him.

'What do you feed on?'

'Flesh,' said the boy, and he pronounced the word with slow <u>relish</u>, as though he were tasting it.

'Flesh! What flesh?'

'Since it interests you, rabbits, wild-fowl, hares, poultry, lambs in their season, children when I can get any; they're usually too well locked in at night, when I do most of my hunting. It's quite two months since I tasted child-flesh.'

Ignoring this remark, Van Cheele tried to draw the boy onto the subject of possible <u>poaching</u> operations.

'You're talking rather through your hat when you speak of feeding on hares... Our hillside hares aren't easily caught.'

'At night I hunt on four feet,' was the somewhat puzzling response.

'I suppose you mean you hunt with a dog?' suggested Van Cheele.

The boy rolled slowly over onto his back and laughed a weird, low laugh that was pleasantly like a chuckle and disagreeably like a snarl...

Van Cheele's artist friend has also seen the boy...

Suddenly I became aware of a naked boy, a bather from some neighbouring pool, I thought, who was standing out on the bare hillside also watching the sunset... Just then the sun dipped out of view, and all the orange and pink slid out of the landscape, leaving it cold and grey. And at the same moment an <u>astounding</u> thing happened – the boy <u>vanished</u> too!'

'What! Vanished away into nothing?' asked Van Cheele excitedly.

'No, that is the dreadful part of it,' answered the artist. On the open hillside where the boy had been standing a second ago, stood a large wolf, blackish in colour, with gleaming fangs and cruel, yellow eyes...

Saki (H H Munro)

COMPREHENSION

A Choose the best answer for each question.

1 When Van Cheele meets the boy he is walking:
   a on the beach   **b** through a wood   **c** in town

2 The boy said he:
   a didn't sleep at night   **b** slept well at night   **c** sleepwalked

3 Van Cheele said that the hares were:
   a caught with dogs   **b** not easily caught   **c** easily caught

4 The boy said that he hunted:
   a with a dog   **b** during the day   **c** on four feet

5 Van Cheele's artist friend saw the wolf:
   a before sunset   **b** during sunset   **c** after sunset

Unit 1 There are more things in heaven and earth / fiction

B 1 Why does Van Cheele think the boy hunts with a dog?

2 How do you think the writer wants you to feel when he writes that the boy feeds on 'child-flesh'?

3 Do you think the boy is frightened of Van Cheele or not? Why?

4 What do you think Van Cheele means when he says to the boy, 'You're rather talking through your hat'?

5 List the five adjectives which the writer uses to describe the wolf.

C Write a sentence or two to explain what you think happens to the boy.

VOCABULARY

Use a dictionary and the context of the passage to explain the meanings of these words. They are underlined in the passage. The first one is done for you.

1 hail = *come*
2 irritated
3 relish
4 poaching
5 astounding
6 vanished

SPELLING

ie / ei

These are the rules to help you choose **ie** or **ei**.
 i before e
 except after c   when the sound is *ee*

So:
- i before e   eg *pi**e**ce*
- except after c   eg *rec**ei**ve*
- when the sound is **not** *ee* eg *v**ie**w*

Copy these headings and put the words in the box under the correct heading. The first one is done for you.

ie = ee sound   ei = follows c   ei = not ee sound
thief

thief	shield	chief	eight	their
rein	brief	field	deceive
deceit	heir	shriek	priest

Gabriel-Ernest

Activity / **1.3**

GRAMMAR AND PUNCTUATION

> **Conjunctions** are words we use to join sentences. The most common conjunctions are *and* and *but*.
>
> We use 'and' when something is expected.
> eg The day was hot. The boy was sunning himself.
>   The day was hot **and** the boy was sunning himself.
>
> We use 'but' when something is unexpected.
> eg He looked like an ordinary boy. He said he ate children!
>   He looked like an ordinary boy **but** he said he ate children!

A Copy these sentences and join them with *and* or *but*. The first one is done for you.

1 Van Cheele saw the boy. He stopped and spoke to him.

  Van Cheele saw the boy and he stopped and spoke to him.

2 The boy said he caught hares. Hares were not easy to catch.

3 The water was very cold. The boy dived in.

4 The boy was standing on the hill. He was watching the sunset.

5 The sun had disappeared. It was cold and grey.

6 He could not see the boy. He could see a large wolf.

> **HINT**
> When you join sentences you don't need the first full stop or the second capital letter.

B Use the conjunctions in the box to complete the sentences below. The first one is done for you.

| and | but | so | because | or |

1 The boy was laid on the rock *but* he was not asleep.

2 The boy was not worried _____ frightened when Van Cheele spoke to him.

3 He lived in the woods _____ he had nowhere else to go.

4 Van Cheele _____ his friend had seen the strange boy.

5 The world turned cold and grey _____ the sun had set.

6 Van Cheele was puzzled _____ he asked his friend about the boy.

Unit 1 There are more things in heaven and earth / fiction

Gabriel-Ernest

Activity / **1.3**

WRITING

Writing descriptions

Good descriptions need adjectives! The adjectives you choose will make your readers feel how you want them to feel, eg *frightened, sad, curious*

Language features

Adjectives

Adjectives appeal to the five senses.

Think carefully about what something:

- looks like
- feels like
- smells like
- sounds like
- tastes like.

Copy and complete the box below with interesting adjectives.

Description of a wolf:	adjectives
sight	
touch	
smell	
hearing	

Dominant impression

How do you want your readers to feel when they have read your description?

Van Cheele's friend is obviously horrified. He says that seeing the wolf was '*dreadful*'.

How would you feel seeing a boy change into:

'*a large wolf, blackish in colour, with gleaming fangs and cruel, yellow eyes*'?

Writing assignment

Use your imagination and write a description of the boy as he turned into a wolf.

Think carefully about how these things changed:

- his eyes
- his hands and feet
- his face
- his teeth
- the way he stands
- his body.

The picture on the opposite page will help you.

Unit 2 I have a dream / fiction

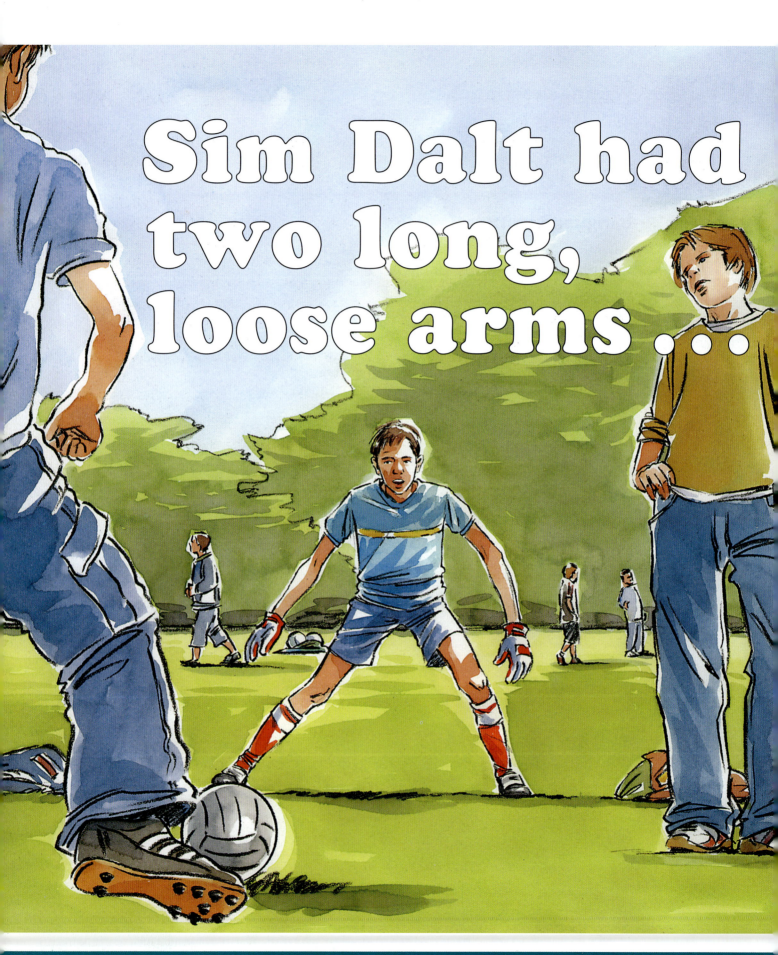

Sim Dalt had two long, loose arms...

The Goalkeeper's Revenge

Extract / 2.1

The story begins...

Sim Dalt had two long, loose arms, <u>spindly</u> legs, a bony face with gleaming brown eyes, and, from the age of twelve, was reckoned to be a bit touched in the head.

Goalkeeping was the main interest in Sim's life. In his nursery days the one indoor pastime that satisfied him was when his mother kicked a rubber ball from the living-room into the kitchen, while Sim stood goal at the middle door. It was rare even then that he let one pass.

He later attended Scuttle Street <u>elementary</u> school, where he was always gnawed with the <u>ferocious</u> wish for four o'clock, when he could dash to the cinder park to play goalie for some team or other. Even in the hot summer days, Sim would <u>cajole</u> a few non-players into a game of football. 'Shoot 'em in, chaps,' he would yell, after lovingly arranging the heaps of jackets for the goalposts, 'the harder the better.'

At twelve he was picked as a goalkeeper for his school team. 'If you let any easy 'uns through,' the captain, Bob Thropper, threatened him, 'I'll bust your shins in!'

But he had no need to warn Sim, for it was rare indeed that anyone could get a ball past him.

It was near the end of the season, and Scuttle Street were at the top of the league and in the final for the Mayor's Shield, when a new and very <u>thorough</u> inspector visited the school. He found Sim's scholastic ability to be of such a low order that he directed him at once to Clinic Street special school.

'I suppose you could continue to play for us until the end of the season,' said Mr Speckle, at a meeting of the team, 'and then, at least, you'll be sure of a medal.'

'What, sir!' <u>interposed</u> Bob Thropper. 'A *cracky school* lad play for us? Ee, sir, that *would* be out of order!'

'But what shall we do for a goalkeeper?' asked the teacher.

'Goalkeepers!' snorted Bob. 'I could buy 'em and sell 'em.'

Bill Naughton

COMPREHENSION

A Copy these sentences. Fill in the missing words.

1. Sim's main interest was being a _ _ _ _ _ _ _ _ _ _.
2. Sim wanted to play football even in the _ _ _ _ _ _.
3. He used heaps of _ _ _ _ _ _ _ for the goalposts.
4. He was _ _ _ _ _ _ when he was picked for the school team.
5. If he played until the end of the season, he would get a _ _ _ _ _.

Unit 2   I have a dream / fiction

B 1 List the adjectives used in the first paragraph to describe Sim.
   2 How do you know he was good at goalkeeping from an early age?
   3 Explain in your own words:
      a 'touched in the head'   b 'In his nursery days'   c 'scholastic ability'.
   4 How did the inspector's decision affect Sim?
   5 Explain in your own words Bob's attitude to goalkeepers.

C Read the first paragraph. If the story had no title and there were no pictures, what would you think it was going to be about?

VOCABULARY

Use a dictionary to explain the meaning of the following words. They are underlined in the passage. The first one is done for you.

1 spindly = thin and weak   2 elementary   3 ferocious
4 cajole   5 thorough   6 interposed

SPELLING

> A **prefix** is a group of letters put at the beginning of a word to change its meaning.
>
> eg **re** + arrange = **re**arrange   to arrange again
>
> **dis** + continue = **dis**continue   not to continue

Choose the prefix ⟦ dis   un   re ⟧ to solve the clues.
The first one is done for you.

1 interested   having no interest   = disinterested
2 satisfied   not being satisfied = _____
3 visit   to visit again   = _____
4 sure   not sure   = _____
5 even   not even   = _____
6 attended   not attended   = _____

HINT
Just add the prefix! Don't miss out any letters.

24

The Goalkeeper's Revenge

Activity / **2.1**

GRAMMAR AND PUNCTUATION

Sentence types

> A sentence is a group of words which makes sense.
> eg sentence   = 'Goalkeeping was the main interest in Sim's life.'
>   not a sentence = Goalkeeping was the main
>
> **Statements** are sentences which tell us something. They end with a full stop.
> eg **S**im was very good at goalkeeping**.**

A Copy and punctuate these statements correctly. The first one is done for you.

1 sim attended Scuttle Street elementary school
   Sim attended Scuttle Street elementary school.

2 he would play football even in the hot summer

3 it was rare anyone got the ball past Sim

HINT

All sentences begin with capital letters.

> **Questions** are sentences which ask us something. They end with a question mark.
> eg '**B**ut what shall we do for a goalkeeper**?**'

B Copy and punctuate these questions correctly. The first one is done for you.

1 what was the main interest in Sim's life
   What was the main interest in Sim's life?

2 did his mum play football with him

3 were Scuttle Street the top of the league

> Sentences which are **exclamations** show when a character is shouting, surprised, frightened etc. They end with an exclamation mark.
> eg 'I'll bust your shins in!'

C Copy and punctuate these exclamations correctly. The first one is done for you.

1 sim's schoolwork was dreadful
   Sim's schoolwork was dreadful!

2 goal

3 if I don't play, I won't get a medal

Unit 2 I have a dream / fiction

The Goalkeeper's Revenge

Activity / 2.1

WRITING

Story openings

> The **beginning** of a story must make the reader want to go on reading. You can begin your story with:
> - a description of the setting
> - a description of a character
> - a conversation.

Language features

Writing in the third person

Many stories are told by a 'narrator'. The narrator is not a character in the story. The narrator:

- tells what is happening in the story = the plot
- writes about the people in the story = the characters
- describes where the story takes place = the setting.

HINT
The narrator is the story teller.

The story opening

It is a good idea to write an interesting story opening which does not tell the reader everything at the very beginning.

The first paragraph of *The Goalkeeper's Revenge* is about Sim but it doesn't mention goalkeeping or football. We have to read on to see if:

- Sim is the goalkeeper in the title
- another character is the goalkeeper
- what the goalkeeper's 'revenge' is!

The writer begins by describing Sim and we want to go on reading after we are told that he '*was reckoned to be a bit touched in the head*'!

Writing assignment

Write the first two paragraphs of a story where:

<u>the first paragraph</u>
- introduces a character
- gives the reader a description of that character

<u>the second paragraph tells us</u>
- what that character's only interest in life is
- how he/she became so interested.

It can be as unusual as you like. Does your character want to be:
- an astronaut?
- a magician?
- a deep-sea diver?

You don't have to choose one of these. You can think of your own idea.

27

Unit 2 I have a dream / fiction

Last night I dreamt...

Rebecca

Extract / 2.2

The story begins...

Last night I dreamt I went to Manderley again. It seemed to me I stood by the iron gate leading to the drive, and for a while I could not enter for the way was <u>barred</u> to me. There was a padlock and a chain upon the gate. I called in my dream to the lodge-keeper, and had no answer, and peering closer through the rusted spokes of the gate I saw that the lodge was <u>uninhabited</u>.

No smoke came from the chimney, and the little lattice windows gaped forlorn. Then, like all dreamers, I was possessed of a sudden with <u>supernatural</u> powers and passed like a spirit through the barrier before me. The drive wound away in front of me, twisting and turning as it had always done, but as I advanced I was aware that a change had come upon it; it was narrow and unkept, not the drive that we had known ...

On and on, now east now west, wound the poor thread that once had been our drive. Sometimes I thought it lost, but it appeared again, beneath a fallen tree perhaps, or struggling on the other side of a muddied ditch created by the winter rains. I had not thought the way so long. Surely the miles had multiplied, even as the trees had done, and the path led but to a <u>labyrinth</u>, some choked wilderness, and not to the house at all. I came upon it suddenly; the approach masked by the unnatural growth of a vast shrub that spread in all directions, and I stood, my heart thumping in my breast, the strange prick of tears behind my eyes.

There was Manderley, our Manderley, secretive and silent as it had always been, the grey stone shining in the moonlight of my dream, the <u>mullioned</u> windows reflecting the green lawns and the terrace. Time could not wreck the perfect symmetry of those walls, nor the site itself, a jewel in the hollow of a hand.

The terrace sloped to the lawns, and the lawns stretched to the sea, and turning I could see the sheet of silver, <u>placid</u> under the moon, like a lake undisturbed by wind or storm...

Moonlight can play odd tricks upon the fancy, even upon a dreamer's fancy. As I stood there, hushed and still, I could swear that the house was not an empty shell but lived and breathed as it had lived before.

Light came from the windows, the curtains blew softly in the night air, and there, in the library, the door would stand half open as we had left it, with my handkerchief on the table beside the bowl of autumn roses.

Daphne du Maurier

COMPREHENSION

A Write 'true' or 'false' for each of these statements.

1. The gate was locked with a padlock and chain.
2. Smoke was coming from the chimney.
3. Manderley was built of yellow stone.
4. In the dream it was daylight.
5. The house was near the sea.

Unit 2 I have a dream / fiction

B 1 How do you know that the dreamer had been to Manderley before?

2 Are the gardens neat or untidy? How do you know?

3 Find the adjective which describes:
   a the spokes of the gate   **b** the ditch   **c** the roses.

4 How does the dreamer feel when she sees the house? Why do you think she feels this way?

5 How are the last two paragraphs different to what had been described before?

C Does the opening of this story make you want to read on or not? Give your reasons.

VOCABULARY

Use a dictionary and the context of the passage to explain the following words. They are underlined in the passage. The first one is done for you.

1 barred = *closed*   2 uninhabited   3 supernatural

4 labyrinth   5 mullioned   6 placid

SPELLING

> A **prefix** is a group of letters put at the beginning of a word to change its meaning. Many prefixes make the word into its opposite.
>
> eg inhabited   **un** + inhabited = **un**inhabited
>
>   natural   **un** + natural   = **un**natural

A Choose a prefix from the box to make each of the following words into its opposite. The first one is done for you.

   un   mis   dis   im

1 tidy *untidy*   2 appear   3 possible

4 count   5 wrap   6 moral

7 obey   8 lead   9 true

HINT
Remember! Just add the prefixes. Don't leave out any letters.

B Use three of the words you have made in sentences of your own.

Rebecca

Activity / **2.2**

GRAMMAR AND PUNCTUATION

Subject and verb

> Every sentence has a **subject**.
> The subject is the person, place or thing that the sentence is about.
>
> Every sentence has a **verb**.
> The verb is what the subject is doing.
>
> eg <u>I</u> called through the gate.
>   subject verb
>
>   <u>The house</u> was silent and empty.
>   subject   verb

A Copy each sentence. Underline the subject. Circle the verb. The first one is done for you.

1 I (had) a wonderful dream.
2 The drive wound away in front of me.
3 The house was secret.
4 The grey stone shone in the moonlight.
5 Light came from the windows.
6 My handkerchief lay on the table.

> **HINT**
> Remember that words like 'was', 'is', 'were' and 'had' are verbs.

B Write sentences using these pairs of subject and verb. The first one is done for you.

1 subject = tree   verb = grew

   The <u>tree grew</u> over to one side.

2 subject = lake   verb = was shining
3 subject = the drive   verb = was
4 subject = moonlight   verb = peeped
5 subject = roses   verb = were
6 subject = I   verb = cried

Unit 2 I have a dream/fiction

Rebecca

Activity / **2.2**

WRITING

Story openings

> You need an interesting start to your story so that the reader will want to 'read on'.
>
> The **opening** of *Rebecca* is very mysterious.
> It leaves you asking:
>
> Who is the dreamer?   Why is the house deserted?

Language features

Writing in the first person

A story can be very boring if every sentence begins with 'I'. Think about:

- changing the order of the words, eg
  I dreamt last night I went to Manderley again.
  '**Last night** I dreamt I went to Manderley again.'

- using conjunctions to join sentences, eg
  I called in my dream to the lodge-keeper. I had no answer.
  '*I called in my dream to the lodge-keeper **and** had no answer.*'

HINT

See how many 'I's you can get rid of.

Adjectives and adjectival phrases

Read these two sentences:

1 The house stood on the edge of the wood.

2 The house, which was ruined and deserted, stood on the edge of a dark, forbidding wood.

Which do you think is better? Why?

Writing assignment

Write a story opening which begins with a dream. Remember:

- write in the first person
- the dream can be real or imaginary
- in the dream you visit a place from your past
- the place can be frightening or welcoming
- use adjectives and adjectival phrases to describe the place
- don't begin every sentence with 'I'.

Unit 2 I have a dream /fiction

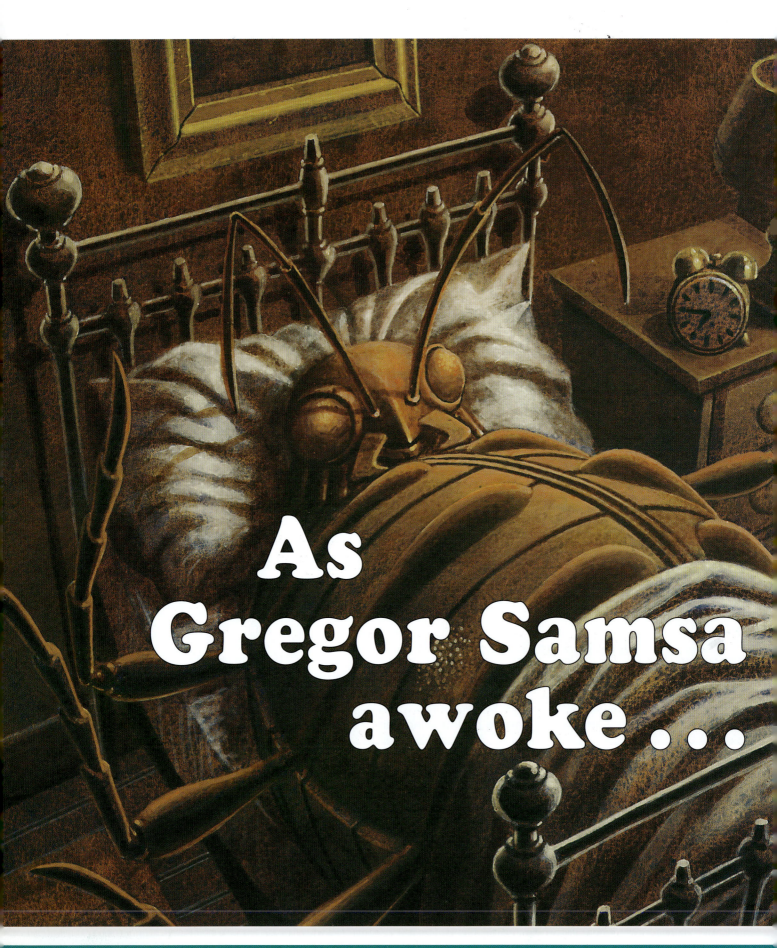

Metamorphosis

Extract / 2.3

The story begins...

As Gregor Samsa awoke one morning from <u>uneasy</u> dreams he found himself <u>transformed</u> in his bed into a gigantic insect. He was lying on his hard, as it were armour-plated, back and when he lifted his head a little he could see his dome-like brown belly divided into stiff arched <u>segments</u> on top of which the bed-quilt could hardly keep in position and was about to slide off completely. His numerous legs, which were pitifully thin compared to the rest of his bulk, waved helplessly before his eyes.

What has happened to me? he thought. It was no dream. His room, a regular human bedroom, only rather too small, lay quiet between the four familiar walls...

Gregor's eyes turned next to the window, and the overcast sky – one could hear raindrops beating on the window gutter – made him quite <u>melancholy</u>. What about sleeping a little longer and forgetting all this nonsense, he thought, but it could not be done, for he was accustomed to sleep on his right side and in his present condition he could not turn himself over. However violently he forced himself towards his right side he always rolled on to his back again. He tried it at least a hundred times, shutting his eyes to keep from seeing his struggling legs, and only <u>desisted</u> when he began to feel in his side a faint dull ache he had never experienced before...

The devil take it all! He felt a slight itching up on his belly; slowly pushed himself on his back nearer to the top of the bed so that he could lift himself more easily, identified the itching place which was surrounded by many small white spots the nature of which he could not understand, and made to touch it with a leg, but drew back immediately, for the contact made a cold shiver run through him...

... the alarm-clock had just struck a quarter to seven – there came a <u>cautious</u> tap at the door behind the head of the bed. 'Gregor,' said a voice – it was his mother's – it's a quarter to seven. Hadn't you a train to catch?'

Franz Kafka

COMPREHENSION

A Choose the best answer.

1 When Gregor woke up he had changed into:
   a a bed quilt   b an insect   c an alarm clock.

2 He was lying on his:
   a back   b belly   c legs.

3 Outside it was:
   a sunny   b snowing   c raining.

4 He was bothered by:
   a a spot   b an itch   c a broken leg.

5 Gregor had to get up to:
   a have a bath   b see his mother   c catch a train.

Unit 2 I have a dream / fiction

B 1 What do you think Gregor might have been dreaming about?
2 What does the adjective *armour-plated* tell you about Gregor's back?
3 Why did Gregor keep rolling onto his back?
4 How did Gregor know that *It was no dream*?
5 What do you think Gregor hoped would happen if he went back to sleep?

C Read the opening sentence carefully. Explain how it makes you feel.

VOCABULARY

Use a dictionary and the context of the extract to explain the meaning of these words. They are underlined in the passage. The first one is done for you.

1 uneasy = frightening   2 transformed   3 segments
4 melancholy   5 desisted   6 cautious

SPELLING

> A **prefix** is a group of letters put at the beginning of a word to change its meaning.
>   eg *pleased*   **dis**pleased
>
> If the last letter of the prefix and the first letter of the word are the same, you will have a double letter.
>   eg di**s** + **s**atisfied = *dissatisfied*
>   i**r** + **r**egular   = *irregular*

A Copy each of these words and add the prefix.

1 **dis** + similar   2 **un** + natural
      + service   + nerve

3 **over** + run   4 **im** + modest
       + rule   + mature

HINT
Each word you make will have a double letter.

> **al** is a prefix meaning 'the whole thing'. It comes from 'all'. When you add it to the front of a word, you leave out one 'l'.
>   eg all + most = **almost**

B Add the prefix **al** to these words.

1 ready   2 though   3 together
4 so   5 ways

Metamorphosis

Activity / **2.3**

GRAMMAR AND PUNCTUATION

Subject and predicate

> Every sentence has a **subject**.
> The subject is the person, place or thing that the sentence is about.
>   eg *Gregor had been dreaming.*
>   *Gregor* = subject
>
> The rest of the sentence is called the **predicate**.
>   *had been dreaming* = predicate

A Write the subject of each of these sentences.
   The first one is done for you.

		Subject
1	He was changed into a giant insect.	He
2	His legs were very thin.	
3	The bedroom was too small.	
4	Gregor thought he should go back to sleep.	
5	He felt a dull ache in his side.	
6	The time was a quarter to seven.	

B Copy the subject and the verb from each of these sentences.
   The first one is done for you.

		Subject	Verb
1	Gregor opened his eyes.	Gregor	opened
2	He had a bad dream.		
3	His belly was itching.		
4	All of his legs waved about.		
5	The alarm clock was beside the bed.		
6	His mother tapped on the door.		

Unit 2 I have a dream / fiction

Metamorphosis

Activity / **2.3**

WRITING

Story openings

The **opening** of this story is very strange.
Waking up as a giant insect is not something that happens every day!

Language features

First sentence

'As Gregor Samsa awoke one morning from uneasy dreams he found himself transformed in his bed into a giant insect.'

This first sentence is so unusual that it 'grabs' the reader's attention.

Writing in the third person

This is not happening to the narrator. It is happening to one of the characters. The narrator used the third person.

    eg 'he'   'him'   'his'

He lets us know what Gregor is thinking and feeling.

Contrast

The writer tells us about the extraordinary thing.

    ie Gregor is a giant insect

and the ordinary things

    ie his room and the weather

Writing assignment

Write the opening of a story where a character wakes up one morning and has been changed into something else!

You should:

- think about something really unusual your character has turned into
- write in the third person
- write an 'attention-grabbing' first sentence
- let the reader know how your character feels about what has happened.

Unit 3 As one great furnace flamed / fiction

Fire in the night...

In Jacqueline Wilson's story The Bed and Breakfast Star, *Elsa and her family have had to move out of their lovely house into a bed and breakfast hotel. One night Elsa realises that the hotel is on fire. She shouts 'FIRE!' over and over again and bangs on people's doors.*

The Bed and Breakfast Star

Extract / 3.1

Then I went charging down the corridor, calling 'FIRE FIRE FIRE!' all over again.

The smoke was stronger now, and I could hear this awful crackling sound down the corridor. One of the men went running towards the kitchen in his pyjamas, but when he got near he slowed down and then backed away.

'Get everyone out! he shouted. The whole kitchen's <u>ablaze</u>. Keep yelling, little kid. Wake them all up, loud as you can.'

I took a huge breath and roared the <u>dreadful</u> warning over and over again. Some people came running out straight away. Others shouted back, and someone started screaming that we were going to be burnt alive.

'No-one will be burnt alive if you just stop <u>panicking</u>,' Mack shouted, charging down the corridor, Pippa under one arm, Hank under the other, Mum stumbling along in her nightie behind them. Mack was only wearing his vest and pants and any other time in the world I'd have rolled around laughing, he looked such a sight.

But we all looked sights. People came <u>blundering</u> out of their bedrooms in nighties and pyjamas and T-shirts and underwear. Some were clutching handbags, some had carrier bags, <u>several</u> had shoved their possessions in blankets and were dragging them along the corridor.

'Leave all your bits and bobs behind. Let's just get out down the stairs. Carry the kids. Come on, get cracking!' Mack yelled. He banged his fist against the fire alarm at the end of the corridor and it started ringing...

We made our way down the stairs, clinging to each other. There was no smoke down on the lower floors but people were still panicking, <u>surging</u> out and running like mad, pushing and shoving. One little kid fell down but his mum pulled him up again and one of the men popped him on his shoulders out of harm's way. The stairs seem to go on for ever, as if we were going down right into the middle of the earth, but at last the lino changed to the cord carpeting of the first floor and then even though our feet kept trying to run downwards, we were on the level of the ground floor.

Jacqueline Wilson

COMPREHENSION

A Copy these sentences. Fill in the missing words.

1. One of the men went running towards the kitchen in his _ _ _ _ _ _ _.
2. The whole kitchen was _ _ _ _ _ _.
3. Mack banged his _ _ _ _ against the fire alarm.
4. There was no _ _ _ _ _ on the lower floors.
5. Most people were _ _ _ _ _ _ _ _ _.

Unit 3 As one great furnace flamed / fiction

B 1 What do you think may have caused the fire? Think carefully about where it started.

  2 In what three ways did people react when they knew there was a fire?

  3 Why do you think Mack was carrying Pippa and Hank?

  4 Find two examples in the extract to show that Mack took charge of the situation.

  5 How would you describe the way the narrator behaved during the fire?

C Write a few sentences to show how the writer builds up the feeling of fear and confusion.

VOCABULARY

Use a dictionary and the context of the story to explain the following words. They are underlined in the passage. The first one is done for you.

1 ablaze = *on fire*   2 dreadful   3 panicking

4 blundering   5 several   6 surging

SPELLING

> The **suffixes ing** and **ed** change the tense of a verb.
>   eg to yell: *She is yell**ing**.* present tense
>   *She yell**ed**.*   past tense
>
> To add **ing** or **ed** to a short verb, look at the letter before the last one:
> - if it is a vowel, double the last letter before adding **ing** or **ed**
>   eg *drag   dra**gg**ing   dra**gg**ed*
> - if it is a consonant, don't double
>   eg *pu**s**h   pushing   pushed*

A Add **ing** and **ed** to each of these short verbs. The first one is done for you.

1 climb / *climbing* / *climbed* 2 step   3 lock   4 look

5 paint   6 rush   7 pull   8 bang

> To add **ing** or **ed** to words ending in 'e', we usually drop the 'e' first.
>   eg *charge   charg**ing**   charg**ed***

B Add **ing** and **ed** to each of these verbs. The first one is done for you.

1 crackle / *crackling* / *crackled* 2 stumble   3 shove   4 move

5 dive   6 hope   7 choke   8 blaze

The Bed and Breakfast Star

Activity / **3.1**

GRAMMAR AND PUNCTUATION

Simple and compound sentences

> A **simple sentence** is made up of one main clause and makes sense by itself.
>
> eg 'I took a huge breath.'
>
> A **compound sentence** is made up of two simple sentences joined by a conjunction.
>
> eg simple sentence = 'I took a huge breath.'
>   simple sentence = 'I roared the dreadful warning.'
>   compound sentence =
>
> 'I took a huge breath (and) roared the dreadful warning.'
>   main clause   conjunction   main clause

A Copy these compound sentences. Underline the two main clauses and put a ring around the conjunction. The first one has been done for you.

1 <u>I went charging down the corridor</u> (and) <u>shouted FIRE!</u>
2 The smoke was stronger now and I could hear a crackling sound.
3 One of the men was near to the kitchen but he backed away.
4 Some people shouted back and someone screamed.
5 There was no smoke on the lower floors but people were still panicking.

B Join each pair of simple sentences to make a compound sentence. Use the conjunctions in the box. The first one is done for you.

| but | although | because | so | and |

1 Mack carried the children.
  Mum stumbled along behind.

  Mack carried the children and Mum stumbled along behind.

2 Some people had carrier bags.
  Some people dragged their things in a blanket.

3 He was only wearing his vest and pants.
  He did not have time to get dressed.

4 He banged the fire alarm.
  The fire brigade would arrive.

5 We managed to make our way downstairs.
  Everyone was panicking.

> **HINT**
>
> When you join the simple sentences you do not need the first full stop and the second capital letter.

Unit 3   As one great furnace flamed / fiction

The Bed and Breakfast Star

Activity / **3.1**

WRITING

A crisis situation

> In many stories, there is usually a 'high point' where the characters find themselves in a difficult situation. This is called a **crisis**.
>
> In the extract the narrator finds herself in a 'crisis situation' when a fire breaks out in the hotel.

Language features

Writing in the first person

In *The Bed and Breakfast Star*, the author writes in the first person. That means she is writing as if she is a character in the story.

When you write in the first person try not to begin every sentence with 'I'. Think about:

- changing the order of the words
- using conjunctions to join sentences.

The impression the writer creates

The reader can feel the panic and confusion by the words and phrases the author chooses, eg

'FIRE FIRE FIRE!'
'awful crackling sound'
'charging down the corridor'
'panicking, surging out'
'running like mad'

These words are used instead of *said*.

Can you think of any others?

How does it end?

In this extract, all the characters reach the ground floor and safety. Not all crisis points in stories end happily. Decide if your crisis is going to end happily or tragically.

Writing assignment

Write a short story which has a crisis.

- You are one of the characters but you do not cause the crisis.
- Write in the first person.

Plan your story by deciding:

- what other characters are involved with you in the crisis
- what the crisis is
- how the crisis ends.

Write three paragraphs: Paragraph 1: the start of the crisis
Paragraph 2: the middle of the crisis
Paragraph 3: the end of the crisis

HINT

Don't begin every sentence with 'I'.

Unit 3 As one great furnace flamed / fiction

After my mum had gone...

The narrator of the story is not allowed to have fireworks and go to the bonfire he and his friends are building. He tells his friends that his mum is going to buy him fireworks that day but they do not believe him. On his way home, he meets a lad in the park and swaps his bike for a bag of fireworks.

After my mum had gone, I went outside and got the bag of fireworks. I was looking at them in the front room when the doorbell rang. It couldn't have been my mum because she's got a key, but I put the fireworks in a cupboard just in case and went to answer it. Norbert, Barry and Tony were standing there. Barry looked at the others, then looked at me with a kind of smile.

'We saw your mum going up Deardon Street. She said you were at home.'

I didn't say anything. I just looked at them. Norbert sniffed.

'Yeah. So we thought we'd come and

The Firework Display

Extract / 3.2

look at your fireworks.'

Norbert grinned his stupid grin. I could've hit him, but I didn't have to.

'You don't believe I've got any fireworks, do you?'

Tony and Barry didn't say anything. Norbert did.

'No!'

'I'll show you.'

I took them into the front room, and got the bag of fireworks out of the cupboard. I put them on the carpet, and we all kneeled round to have a look. They were really impressed, especially Norbert.

'Blooming hummer, did your mum buy you all these?'

'Course. I told you.'

Norbert kept picking one up after the other.

'But there's everything. Look at these dive-bombers. And look at the size of these rockets!'

Tony picked up an electric storm.

'These are great. They go on for ages.'

The three of them kept going through all the fireworks. They just couldn't believe it. I felt really chuffed.

'I'd better put them away now.'

Norbert had taken out a sparkler.

'I've never seen sparklers as big as these. Let's light one.'

'No, I'm putting them away now.'

I wanted to get rid of Barry, Tony and Norbert, and see if I could find that lad in the park. I'd proved I'd got my own fireworks now. I'd make up some excuse for not coming to the bonfire on Monday, but none of them could say I hadn't been given my own fireworks. None of them could say that, now.

'Go on, light a sparkler, just one. They're quite safe.'

Well, what harm could it do? Just one sparkler. I got the matches from the mantelpiece, and Norbert held it while I lit it. When it got going, I took hold of it, and we sat round in a circle and watched it sparkle away. Suddenly, Tony screamed.

I looked down and saw lots of bright colours. For a split second I couldn't move. I was paralysed.

Suddenly, fireworks were flying everywhere. Bangers went off, rockets were flying. Sparks were shooting up to the ceiling. It was terrifying. Norbert hid behind the sofa, and Tony stood by the door, while Barry and me tried to put the fireworks out by stamping on them.

George Layton

COMPREHENSION

A Write 'true' or 'false' for each of these statements.

1. The narrator and his mum looked at the bag of fireworks.
2. Norbert, Barry and Tony came to look at the fireworks.
3. Norbert suggested they light a sparkler.
4. The bonfire was on Tuesday.
5. Barry stamped on the fireworks.

Unit 3 As one great furnace flamed / fiction

B 1 How did the boys know the narrator was at home?
2 Five types of fireworks are named in the extract. What are they?
3 What did the boys:
   a see when the fireworks went off?
   b hear when the fireworks went off?
4 How did each of the boys react when the fireworks went off?
5 Explain in your own words how you think the accident happened.

C How do you think the writer wanted you to feel when the fireworks went off accidentally?

VOCABULARY

Use a dictionary and the context of the passage to explain these words. They are underlined in the passage. The first one is done for you.

1 grinned = *smiled stupidly*   2 impressed   3 especially
4 chuffed   5 paralysed   6 terrifying

SPELLING

> **Homophones** are words which sound the same but have different spellings and different meanings.
>   eg *Did your mum **buy** you all these?*
>   *Tony stood **by** the door.*

Find the homophone in the extract for each of these words. The clues will help you. The first one has been done for you.

homophone	clue	
1 bean	past tense of to be	been
2 sore	past tense of to see	_ _ _
3 hymn	opposite of her	_ _ _
4 grate	wonderful	_ _ _ _ _
5 sea	your eyes do this	_ _ _
6 sum	a number of	_ _ _ _
7 quay	you lock a door with this	_ _ _

48

The Firework Display

Activity / **3.2**

GRAMMAR AND PUNCTUATION

Complex sentences

> Remember! A **simple sentence** makes sense on its own.
> eg *I looked down.*
>
> A **compound sentence** is two or more simple sentences joined by a conjunction.
> eg simple sentence: '*I looked down.*'
>   simple sentence: '*I saw lots of bright colours.*'
>   compound sentence: '*I looked down* **and** *saw lots of bright colours.*'

A Join these simple sentences to make compound sentences. The first one is done for you.

1 I went outside.   I got the bag of fireworks.

   I went outside and I got the bag of fireworks.

2 I had lots of fireworks.   Norbert didn't believe me.

3 Should we light a sparkler?   Should we set off a banger?

4 I got the matches.   I could light the fireworks.

5 We stamped on the fireworks.   They didn't stop burning.

HINT

Don't use 'and' every time!

> A **complex sentence** is made up of a simple sentence and phrases. The phrases do not make sense on their own.
> eg *The fireworks went off, flying around the room.*
> The phrase *flying around the room* does not make sense on its own.

B Add a phrase beginning with an 'ing' word to make these simple sentences into complex sentences. The first one is done for you.

1 Norbert stood there, _____.

   Norbert stood there, grinning stupidly.

2 I looked at the bag of fireworks, _____.

3 The rocket shot up, _____.

4 Norbert hid behind the sofa, _____.

5 Mum came through the door, _____.

Unit 3 As one great furnace flamed / fiction

The Firework Display

Activity / **3.2**

WRITING

A crisis

> A **crisis** is a time of difficulty or great danger.
> When the sparkler set fire to the other fireworks, it was a crisis for the narrator and his friends.
> The crisis in the extract is an accident but the narrator and his friends are to blame.

Language features

Writing in the first person

This story is written by one of the characters in the story. What happens is happening to him and his friends.

Description

For the reader to feel that the boys are scared and panicking, the writer paints a vivid picture of what is happening. Look at these two descriptions.

| The fireworks went off. | The fireworks went off. Suddenly, the fireworks were flying everywhere. Bangers went off, rockets were flying. Sparks were shooting up to the ceiling. It was terrifying. |

Which description do you think is better? Why?

Imagine you were writing a story where a water pipe had burst. Improve this description:

> There was water coming through the ceiling.

How does the crisis end?

In the extract, we do not find out what happened after the crisis. It is a 'cliff-hanger'. We have to read on to see what happens. Sometimes it is a good idea to end your story on a crisis. The reader has to imagine what might happen.

Writing assignment

Write a short story where there are:
- three characters
- a crisis caused by one of the characters.

Think about:
- how the crisis is caused
- what the characters do
- where to end the story so that your reader has to imagine what happens next.

Unit 3 As one great furnace flamed / fiction

We'll build a pile...

A group of boys of different ages has been stranded on an island after a plane crash. The pilot was the only adult with them and he has died. The boys have to look after themselves and try to stay alive until help comes. One of Ralph's ideas is to light a big fire that a passing plane or ship might see. He has spotted an area of rotting wood they could use.

'We'll build a pile. Come on.'

They found the likeliest path down and began tugging at the dead wood. And the small boys who had reached the top came sliding too till everyone but Piggy was busy. Most of the wood was so rotten that when they pulled it broke up into a shower of <u>fragments</u> and woodlice and decay; but some trunks came out in one piece. The twins, Sam 'n' Eric, were the first to get a likely log but they could do nothing till Ralph, Jack, Simon, Roger and Maurice

Lord of the Flies

Extract / 3.3

found room for a hand-hold. Then they inched the grotesque dead thing up the rock and toppled it over the top. Each party of boys added a quota, less or more, and the pile grew. At the return Ralph found himself alone on a limb with Jack and they grinned at each other, sharing this burden. Once more, amid the breeze, the shouting, the slanting sunlight on the high mountain, was shed that glamour, that strange invisible light of friendship, adventure, and content.

'Almost too heavy.'

Jack grinned back.

'Not for the two of us.'

Together, joined in effort by the burden, they staggered up the last steep of the mountain. Together, they chanted One! Two! Three! and crashed the log on to the great pile. Then they stepped back, laughing with triumphant pleasure, so that immediately Ralph had to stand on his head. Below them, boys were still labouring, though some of the small ones had lost interest and were searching for fruit. Now the twins, with unsuspected intelligence, came up the mountain with armfuls of dried leaves and dumped them against the pile. One by one, as they sensed that the pile was complete the boys stopped going back for more and stood, with the pink, shattered top of the mountain around them. Breath came even now, and sweat dried.

Ralph and Jack looked at each other while society paused about them. The shameful knowledge grew in them and they did not know how to begin confession. Ralph spoke first, crimson in the face.

'Will you?'

He cleared his throat and went on.

'Will you light the fire?'

Now the absurd situation was open, Jack blushed too. He began to mutter vaguely.

'You rub two sticks. You rub –'

He glanced at Ralph, who blurted out the last confession of incompetence.

'Has anyone got any matches?'

William Golding

COMPREHENSION

A Choose the best answer for each question.

1. Most of the wood was:
   a wet   **b** rotten   **c** burnt.

2. Jack was helped with the heavy log by:
   a Ralph   **b** Roger   **c** Maurice.

3. Some of the small boys began to search for:
   a leaves   **b** matches   **c** fruit.

4. Jack thought they could light the fire by rubbing together:
   a logs   **b** sticks   **c** leaves.

5. Ralph was the first to realise that they had no:
   a fruit   **b** rocks   **c** matches.

Unit 3 As one great furnace flamed / fiction

B 1 Why did the boys want to light a fire?

2 Why do you think the twins could do nothing with the log they had found?

3 Do you think Ralph and Jack were:
- enjoying themselves
- not enjoying themselves?

How do you know?

4 Why do you think it was '*intelligent*' of the twins to bring dried leaves?

5 What did Ralph find it hard to confess?

C The boys had gathered a large pile of wood but had no matches. How do you think they could light the fire?

VOCABULARY

Use a dictionary and the context of the extract to explain these words. They are underlined in the passage. The first one is done for you.

1 fragments = *broken pieces*   2 grotesque   3 quota

4 labouring   5 unsuspected   6 absurd

SPELLING

> The letter **c** can make a **soft** sound like 's'.
> eg for**c**e   woodli**c**e
>
> The letter **c** can make a **hard** sound like 'k'.
> eg de**c**ayed   **c**reepers
>
> Learn the rules: If 'c' is followed by and 'e' or an 'i' it is soft.
> If 'c' is followed by any other letter it is hard.

The answers to these clues all have a soft c. Can you solve them?
The first one is done for you.

1 You use this to draw with.   Begins with p and has six letters.   *pencil*

2 This is the last month of the year.   Begins with D and has eight letters.

3 you see films here   Begins with c and has six letters.

4 this is the middle of something   Begins with c and has six letters.

5 to make up your mind   Begins with d and has six letters.

6 the opposite of give   Begins with r and has seven letters.

7 the opposite of war   Begins with p and has five letters.

8 the plural of mouse   Begins with m and has four letters.

GRAMMAR AND PUNCTUATION

Adjectival clauses

> To make our writing more interesting, we can use **adjectives**.
>
> eg 'the **dead** wood'   'the **small** boys'
>
> Adjectives tell us more about nouns.
>
> To give more information about people we can use **adjectival clauses**.
>
> eg Ralph, **who was the leader**, decided that they should make a fire.
>
> The adjectival clause *who was the leader* tells us more about Ralph.

A Copy each sentence and underline the **adjectival clause**.

1. The twins, who were the first to get there, found a likely log.
2. Ralph, who was pleased, stood on his head.
3. Jack, who was pulling his underlip, nodded.

> **HINT**
>
> The adjectival clauses begin with a comma and end with a comma.

B Add **adjectival clauses** to these sentences to give the reader more information.

1. Jack and Ralph _____ grinned at each other.
2. The boys _____ were ready to make the fire.
3. Jack _____ blushed too.

> **HINT**
>
> Begin with 'who'.

> We can use **adjectival clauses** to give more information about things.
>
> eg The wood, **which was rotten**, broke into pieces.
>
> The adjectival clause *which was rotten* tells us more about the wood.

C Copy each sentence and underline the **adjectival clause**.

1. The log, which was too heavy for the twins, had to be carried by the older boys.
2. The pile, which the boys had made, was huge.
3. The fire, which the boys had made, could not be lit.

> **HINT**
>
> Begin with 'which'.

D Add **adjectival clauses** to these sentences to give the reader more information.

1. The trees _____ had fallen over.
2. The pile _____ was nearly finished.
3. The mountain _____ was high and rocky.

Unit 3 As one great furnace flamed / fiction

Lord of the Flies

Activity / **3.3**

WRITING

Complications

> In the extract you have read, the boys have a good idea. They will build a fire and hope that someone will see it and come to save them.
> - The **complication** in the story is that they have not thought about how they will light the fire.
> - The **complication** is the part of the story where everything does not go as planned.
> - A **complication** happens either because:
>   – something unexpected happens
>   – some part of the plan has not been thought about.

Language features

Everything is going too well!

Ralph has the good idea of building a fire. All the boys except Piggy join in and the fire is soon built. The writer tells us how the fire is built in the order that things happen:

1 Ralph spots where the wood can be gathered.
2 The boys find '*the likeliest path*' down the mountain.
3 The boys gather wood and dried leaves and make a huge pile.
4 The boys all '*sensed that the pile was complete*'.
5 They stopped gathering wood.

The complication

The reader is now expecting the boys to light the fire and is surprised when the complication is introduced. They have no matches!

Writing assignment

Write the 'complication' part of a story where a group of people have:
- worked together to achieve something
- cannot finish what they set out to do because they have not planned carefully enough.

In your planning you should:
- decide on the characters involved
- decide what they are trying to do
- write what they do up to the complication
- introduce the complication to surprise your reader.

Unit 4 Red in tooth and claw / poetry

The fox was strong...

Reynard the Fox

Extract / **4.1**

The fox was strong, he was full of running,
He could run for an hour and then be <u>cunning</u>,
But the cry behind him made him chill,
They were nearer now and they meant to kill.
They meant to run him until his blood
<u>Clogged</u> on his heart as his brush with mud.
Till his back bent up and his tongue hung flagging
And his belly and brush were filthed from dragging,
Till he <u>crouched</u> stone-still, dead-beat and dirty,
With nothing but teeth against the thirty.
And all the way to that blinding end
He would meet with men and have none his friend:
Men to <u>holloa</u> and men to run him,
With stones to stagger and yells to stun him;
Men to head him, with whips to beat him;
Teeth to <u>mangle</u> and mouths to eat him.
And all the way, that wild high crying,
To cold his blood with the thought of dying,
The horn and the cheer, and the drum-like thunder
Of the horses-hooves stamping the meadows under.
He <u>upped</u> his brush and went with a will
For the Sarsen Stones on Wan Dyke Hill.

John Masefield

COMPREHENSION

A Copy these sentences. Fill in the missing words.

1 The fox could __ __ __ for an hour.
2 The hunters meant to __ __ __ __ the fox.
3 The fox had nothing but __ __ __ __ __ against the hunters.
4 Men would beat him with their __ __ __ __ __.
5 The fox headed towards the __ __ __ __ __ __ __ __ __ __.

Unit 4 Red in tooth and claw / poetry

B 1 What do you think the poet means when he says the fox was '*full of running*'?

  2 After the fox had been running for a long time what would happen to:
   a his heart
   b his brush
   c his back
   d his tongue
   e his belly?

  3 How do you know the people the fox would meet would be cruel to him?

  4 What would the dogs do to the fox?

  5 What do you think is making:
   a '*that wild high crying*'
   b '*the drum-like thunder*'?

C When you read the poem, how do you feel about:
  a the men   **b** the dogs   **c** the fox?

VOCABULARY

Use a dictionary and the context of the poem to explain these words.
They are underlined in the poem. The first one is done for you.

1 cunning = *crafty*   2 clogged   3 crouched

4 holloa   5 mangle   6 upped

SPELLING

> A **suffix** is a letter or group of letters added to the end of a word.
>
> The suffix **ion** is very common.
> The suffix **ion** usually has an 's' or a 't' in front of it.
>   eg *invade* (verb)   *invas***ion** (abstract noun)

Add 'ion' to each of these verbs. The first one is done for you.

1 to concentrate = *concentration*   2 to create

3 to explain   4 to prepare

5 to decide   6 to tense

7 to divide   8 to add

HINT
Use a dictionary to check your spelling!

Reynard the Fox

Activity / **4.1**

GRAMMAR AND PUNCTUATION

Adjectival clauses

> **Remember:** A simple sentence is made up of one main clause which makes sense:
>
> eg *The hunters chased the fox*.
>   subject   verb   object
>
> **Adjectival clauses** give us more information about the subject:
>
> eg *The hunters, who wore red coats, chased the fox*.
>   adjectival clause
>
> **Remember:** **who** is used for people
> **which** is used for things

A Copy the sentences and add a suitable **adjectival clause** from the box below.

1 The loud barking made his blood go cold.
2 The hunters meant to kill the fox.
3 The men would beat the fox.
4 The Sarsen Stones were on Wan Dyke Hill.
5 His brush was clogged with mud.

HINT
Remember the commas.

which dragged in the dirt	who were getting nearer
who carried whips	which came from the dogs
which the fox was making for	

B Add **adjectival clauses** to these sentences to give the reader more information.

1 The stones, _____, would stun the fox.
2 The hunters, _____, rode huge horses.
3 The dogs, _____, would eat the fox.
4 The horses, _____, could catch up with the fox.
5 The fox, _____, escaped.

Unit 4 Red in tooth and claw / poetry

Reynard the Fox

Activity / **4.1**

WRITING

Narrative poetry

> A **narrative poem** tells a story. Like a story, a narrative poem has:
> - characters
> - a plot
> - a setting.
>
> In this extract from *Reynard the Fox*, the main character is the fox, the setting is the countryside, and the plot is the chase.

Language features

Rhyme

Some poetry rhymes and some does not. In rhyming poetry, the words which rhyme come at the end of the lines. The pattern of rhyme is called the **rhyme scheme**.

You can work out a poem's rhyme scheme like this:

- Look at the last word of the first line — ie *running*. Call it: → A
- Look at the last word of the next line — ie *cunning*. It rhymes with the first line, so it is also: → A
- Look at the last word of the third line — ie *chill*. It doesn't rhyme with the first two, so call it: → B
- Look at the last word of the fourth line — ie *kill*. It rhymes with the third line so it is also: → B

The rhyme scheme for the first four lines of this poem is: A A B B
This rhyme scheme is called **rhyming couplets**.

In *Reynard the Fox*, what will you call:
- lines 5 and 6?
- lines 7 and 8?
- lines 9 and 10?

Writing assignment

Write your own poem about an animal being chased. It could be chased by people or by another animal.
- Write at least ten lines.
- Write in rhyming couplets.

Look at the picture. How do you think the fox is feeling? The animal you write about will feel just like the fox.

Unit 4 Red in tooth and claw / poetry

They stare at you...

Owls

Extract / **4.2**

They stare at you,
these ugly <u>phantoms</u> of the night,
and do not seem to care
if you stare back at them.
All day they <u>perch</u>, half asleep,
in lonely ruins, dark church towers,
not liking the sun,
dozing, and dreaming with stupid face,
of <u>scurrying</u> mice, fat beetles, baby birds,
swallowed greedily in one cruel gulp.

At <u>twilight</u> they come out.
Like floating paper glide along lanes,
noiselessly dipping over hedges,
or fanning their ghostly way
around the houses, down the avenues,
ears and eyes set for the kill.
Then, <u>gorged</u> with fresh meat,
they sag back home,
the moon's eye watching them,
hooting in the wind,
waiting for the next raw victim.

I do not like owls.
I shiver when I hear them
screeching at the bottom of the garden,
<u>invading</u> the darkness,
glad I'm not a mouse,
small bird or beetle.

Leonard Clark

COMPREHENSION

A Write 'true' or 'false' for each of these statements.

1 During the day, the owls are half asleep.
2 Owls like the sun.
3 Owls hunt at night.
4 Owls like their food cooked.
5 The poet likes owls.

Unit 4 Red in tooth and claw / poetry

B 1 Where do the owls perch?

2 What do the owls dream about?

3 The owls are described as moving '*like floating paper*'. Explain in your own words what the poet means.

4 Why do you think the owls '*sag back home*'?

5 The poet says '*I do not like owls*'. Find three adjectives the poet uses to make owls seem unpleasant.

C Imagine you are a small bird or a beetle. Write a few sentences to explain how you feel when you see an owl, '*ears and eyes set for the kill*'.

VOCABULARY

Use a dictionary and the context of the poem to explain these words. They are underlined in the poem. The first one is done for you.

1 phantoms = *ghosts*   2 perch   3 scurrying

4 twilight   5 gorged   6 invading

SPELLING

> One thing = **singular**
> More than one = **plural**
>
> We add 's' to most nouns to make them plurals.
>   eg *owl / owls*   *bird / birds*
>
> If the noun ends in **s sh ch** or **x** we add **es**.
>   eg *fox / foxes*   *church / churches*

Write the plural of these words. The first one is done for you.

1 ruin   *ruins*   2 crash

3 bench   4 face

5 match   6 bush

7 box   8 beetle

9 lane   10 house

11 bus   12 garden

HINT
Look at the last letters of each word.

GRAMMAR AND PUNCTUATION

Noun and verb agreement

Look: *the owl stares*   *the owls stare*
  singular noun 's' on the verb   plural noun no 's' on the verb

So: singular   plural
   I stare   we stare
   you stare   you stare
   he stare**s**   they stare
   she stare**s**
   it stare**s**

A Write the correct form of the verb from the two in brackets to complete each sentence. The first one is done for you.

1 The owls   (perch / perches)   in dark churches.   *perch*
2 One owl   (glide / glides)   along the lane.
3 A mouse   (scurry / scurries) into a hedge.
4 The owl   (swallow / swallows) a beetle.
5 I do not   (like / likes)   owls.
6 The moon   (watch / watches)   the owls.

So that nouns and verbs 'agree' we use:
- **is** and **was** for singular nouns
  eg *The owl is / was ugly.*
- **are** and **were** for plural nouns
  eg *The owls are / were ugly.*

B Copy these sentences, adding **is** or **are**. The first one is done for you.

1 The owls are asleep during the day.
2 The beetles _____ fat.
3 The small bird _____ food for the owl.
4 The owl's eyes _____ looking for something to kill.
5 The owl's screech _____ frightening.

Unit 4 Red in tooth and claw / poetry

Owls

Activity / **4.2**

WRITING

Poetry

In this poem *Owls* the poet is describing the owls and what he dislikes about them. He uses powerful words to help the reader see how ugly and horrible he thinks they are.

Language features

Word choice

The poet really dislikes owls and you can see how strongly he feels about them through the words he chooses to describe them.

They are: 'ugly'   'stupid'   'ghostly'   'gorged'

Present tense

The poet has written in the present tense which makes us feel the owls are here NOW!

They: 'stare'   'perch'   'come out'   'glide'
They are: 'dozing'   'dreaming'   'floating'   'hooting'

Verses

The poem is written in three verses:
  Verse 1: Owls during the day
  Verse 2: Owls at night
  Verse 3: How the poet feels

Writing assignment

Choose an animal which you do not like and write a poem about it.
- Think carefully about the words you choose to describe the animal so the reader knows how you feel.
- Write in the present tense.
- Write three verses:
  Verse 1: the animal is resting
  Verse 2: the animal is active
  Verse 3: explain why you dislike the animal.

Unit 4 Red in tooth and claw / poetry

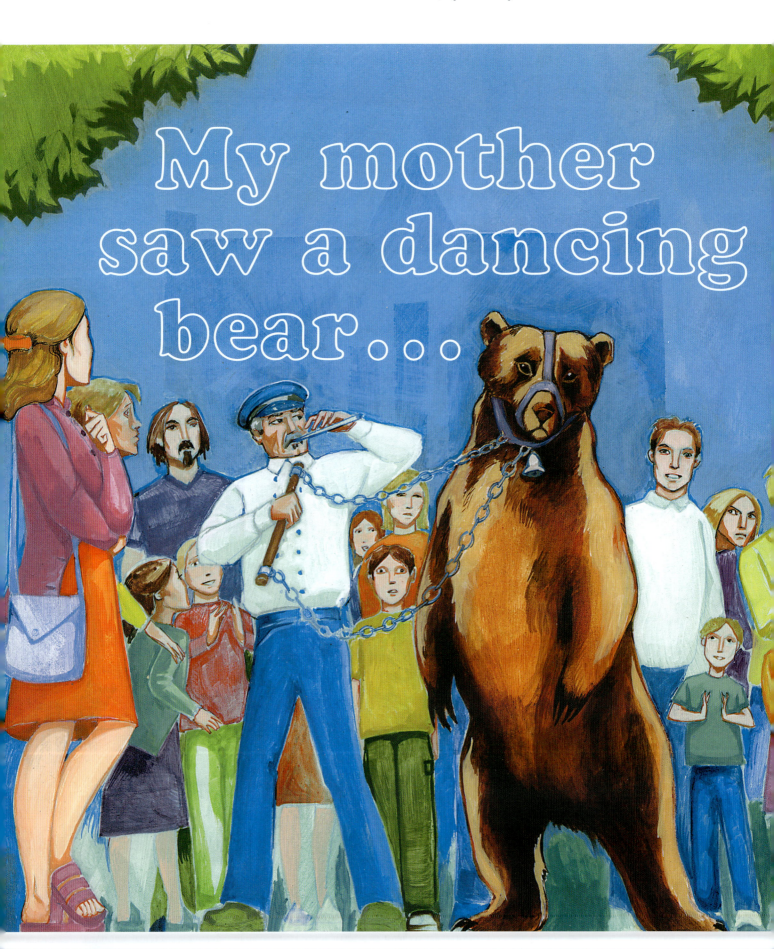

My mother saw a dancing bear

Extract / **4.3**

My mother saw a dancing bear
By the schoolyard, a day in June.
The keeper stood with chain and bar
And <u>whistle-pipe</u>, and played a tune.

And <u>bruin</u> lifted up its head
And lifted up its dusty feet,
And all the children laughed to see
It <u>caper</u> in the summer heat.

They watched as for the Queen it died,
They watched it march. They watched it halt.
They heard the keeper as he cried,
'Now, roly-poly!' '<u>Somersault</u>!'

And then, my mother said, there came
The keeper with the <u>begging</u> cup,
The bear with burning coat of fur,
<u>Shaming</u> the laughter to a stop.

They paid a penny for the dance,
But what they saw was not the show;
Only, in bruin's aching eyes,
Far-distant forests, and the snow.

Charles Causley

COMPREHENSION

A Choose the best answer.

1 When the poet saw the dancing bear, she was in:
   a a zoo   **b** a schoolyard   **c** a forest.

2 The dancing bear visited the town in:
   a June   **b** November   **c** February.

3 The keeper played:
   a a drum   **b** a guitar   **c** a whistle-pipe.

4 The bear had to:
   a sing   **b** play the pipe   **c** march.

5 The begging cup was for:
   a money   **b** food   **c** water.

Unit 4 Red in tooth and claw / poetry

B 1 With what did the keeper control the bear?

2 Give four examples of the things the bear had to do.

3 How much did the people pay to see the bear dance?

4 Why do you think the people were shamed into not laughing?

5 What do you think the bear is thinking about when the poet says:
*'Only, in bruin's aching eyes,
Far distant forests, and the snow.'*

C If you had been watching the bear would you have laughed or been sad, or both? Explain why.

VOCABULARY

Use a dictionary and the context of the poem to explain these words. They are underlined in the poem. The first one has been done for you.

1 whistle-pipe = *musical instrument*   2 bruin   3 caper

4 somersault   5 begging   6 shaming

SPELLING

> **Unstressed vowels** are vowels which we do not sound or do not sound very clearly when we speak.
>
> eg spelt = usu**a**lly
>   said   = *usully* 'a' is unstressed
>   spelt = int**e**rest
>   said   = *intrest* 'e' is unstressed

A Copy these words. Say them to yourself. Circle the **unstressed vowel**. The first one is done for you.

1 parl(i)ament   2 religious   3 estuary

4 vowel   5 mineral   6 literature

B Write the correct spelling of these words. The **unstressed vowel** has been left out. The first one is done for you.

1 temprature = *temperature*   2 marrage

3 labratory   4 funral

5 medcine   6 busness

My mother saw a dancing bear

Activity / 4.3

GRAMMAR AND PUNCTUATION

Punctuating poetry

> The use of **capital letters** and **punctuation** in poetry is different from the way we use it in other types of writing.
> - New lines in poetry often begin with a capital letter.
> - The end of lines can have:
>   - a full stop — to show a definite pause
>   - a comma — to show a brief pause
>   - no punctuation — to show we should read on without stopping
>
> eg '**A**nd bruin lifted up its head
> **A**nd lifted up its dusty feet,
> **A**nd all the children laughed to see
> **I**t caper in the summer heat.'

Copy out the poem below, putting in the capital letters and punctuation where you think they ought to go.

> I watched the bear
> dancing and doing tricks
> looking sad
> the children laughed and
> wanted more
> but I was shamed
> to see the show
> and felt the bear's
> unhappiness
> It should be free
> roaming distant hills
> not tied by a chain
> earning pennies
> from the crowd.

Unit 4 Red in tooth and claw / poetry

My mother saw a dancing bear

Activity / **4.3**

WRITING

Narrative poetry

> A **narrative poem** tells a story. Like a story, a narrative poem has:
> - characters
> - a plot
> - a setting.
>
> In this poem *My mother saw a dancing bear*, the main character is the bear, the setting is the schoolyard, and the plot is the performance of the bear.
>
> However, the poet does not just tell a story. He is making a point about the dancing bear. As we read the poem we feel that the bear is being cruelly treated and it should be in the wild where it belongs.

Language features

Rhyme

The poet has written a rhyming poem. What is the rhyme scheme?

Contrast

The poet makes us think about the situation the bear is in by using contrast.

- In the first three verses we are told of the dancing bear, the tricks it performs and the enjoyment of the audience:

  'And all the children laughed to see
  It caper in the summer heat.'

- The last two verses are a contrast. The mood changes:

  'Shaming the laughter to a stop.'

Writing assignment

Write this narrative poem as if you were the bear. Describe:
- what you do
- how the audience enjoys it.

Finish the poem by describing how you feel.

The picture on the opposite page will help you.

Unit 5 Let slip the dogs of war / fiction

We'll have another game...

The story is set in 1914 at the beginning of the First World War. Four young men, close friends from a Suffolk village, decide they will join the army and be part of the great 'adventure'. Christmas brings the blessed relief of a cease-fire and a spontaneous game of football between the British and German army in No Man's Land.

Some of the British officers took a dim view of such sport, and when the game came to its <u>exhausted</u> end, the men were encouraged back to their trenches for a carol service and supper. The <u>haunting</u> sound of men singing drifted back and forth across No Man's Land in the still night air.

'Good night, Tommies. See you tomorrow.'

'Good night, Fritz. We'll have another game.'

But Boxing Day passed without a game. The officers were alarmed at what had happened on Christmas Day. If such friendly <u>relations</u> continued, how could they get the men to fight again? How could the war continue?...

At dawn a few days later, the Germans <u>mounted</u> a full-scale attack. The friendly Germans from Saxony had been withdrawn and replaced by fresh troops from Prussia. They were met by rapid and deadly fire from the British and were forced back.

War Game

Extract / 5.1

The order was given to counter attack, to try to take the German trenches before they could reorganise themselves. Will and the rest of the soldiers scrambled over the parapet.

Freddie still had the football! He drop-kicked it far into the mist of No Man's Land.

'That'll give someone a surprise,' he said.

'Why are goalies always daft?' thought Will.

They were on the attack. Running in a line, Will in a centre forward position, Lacey to his left, young Billy on the wing.

From the corner of his eye Will saw Freddie dive full-length, then curl up as if clutching a ball in the best goalkeeping tradition.

'Daft as a brush,' Will thought.

Suddenly they all seemed to be tackled at once. The whole line went down. Earth and sky turned over, and Will found himself in a shell hole staring at the sky. Then everything went black.

Slowly the blackness cleared and Will could see the hazy sky once more. Bits of him felt hot and other bits felt very cold. He couldn't move his legs. He heard a slight movement. There was someone else in the shell hole.

Will dimly recognised the gleam of a fixed bayonet and the outline of a German.

'*Wasser. Wasser,*' the German said.

It was about the only German word Will knew. He fumbled for his water-bottle and managed to push it towards the German with the butt of his rifle.

The German drank deeply. He didn't have the strength to return the bottle.

'*Kinder?*' he said. Will shook his head. The German held up three fingers. Will tried to shake his head again to show that he did not understand, but the blackness returned.

Later he saw a pale ball of gold in the misty sky. 'There's a ball in Heaven,' he thought. 'Thank God. We'll all have a game when this nightmare's over.'

At home when he had a bad dream he knew if he opened his eyes, the bad dream would end. But here, his eyes were already open.

Perhaps if he closed them again, the nightmare would end.

He closed his eyes.

Michael Foreman

COMPREHENSION

A Copy these sentences. Fill in the missing words.

1 After the football match, the soldiers went back to their _ _ _ _ _ _ _ _.

2 The Germans mounted a full-scale attack at _ _ _ _.

3 Freddie _ _ _ _ - _ _ _ _ _ _ the football into No Man's Land.

4 When Will was in the shell-hole, he couldn't move his _ _ _ _.

5 Will thought they would have a game when the _ _ _ _ _ _ _ _ _ was over.

Unit 5 Let slip the dogs of war / fiction

B 1 Explain what you think 'No Man's Land' is.

  2 Explain what you think these phrases mean:
    a 'a dim view'   **b** 'full-scale attack'   **c** 'dive full-length'.

  3 What do you think the German was trying to ask Will when he said 'Kinder'?

  4 Will gave the German his water bottle. What does that show you about him?

  5 At the end of the story, do you think Will was really having a nightmare? Explain what you think is happening to him.

C What do you think happened to Freddie and Will after the battle?

VOCABULARY

Use a dictionary and the context of the story to explain these words. They are underlined in the passage. The first one is done for you.

1 exhausted = tired out   2 haunting   3 relations

4 mounted   5 parapet   6 butt

SPELLING

> To make:
> - most nouns plural, add **s**   eg *officer / officer**s***
> - nouns which end in s / ch / sh / x plural, add **es**
>   eg *trench / trench**es***
> - nouns ending in o, usually add **es**   eg *hero / hero**es***
> - nouns ending in f / fe, change to **v** and add **es**
>   eg *half / hal**ves***

A Make these nouns **plural**. The first one is done for you.

  1 order *orders*   2 brush   3 piano   4 fox

> If a noun ends in **y**, follow these rules:
> - If the letter before the y is a vowel (a / e / i / o / u) add **s**
>   eg *boy / boy**s***
> - If the letter before the y is a consonant, change the **y** to **i** and add **es**   eg *army / arm**ies***

B Make these words **plural**. The first one is done for you.

  1 poppy = *poppies*   2 key   3 county   4 sky

War Game

Activity / **5.1**

GRAMMAR AND PUNCTUATION

Powerful verbs

> Verbs are very important types of words for a writer. Choosing **powerful verbs** helps the reader to understand what is going on.
>
> eg *The officers were not just <u>worried</u>, they were 'alarmed'.*
>
> *Will and the rest of the soldiers did not just <u>go</u> over the parapet, they 'scrambled'.*
>
> *He didn't just <u>get</u> his water bottle, he 'fumbled' for it.*

A Use a thesaurus and write three **powerful verbs** which are synonyms for each of these verbs. The first one is done for you.

1 got *received obtained acquired*

2 said   3 took   4 saw

5 asked   6 ate   7 ran

8 liked   9 walked   10 laughed

HINT

A synonym means the same or nearly the same.

B In another part of the story, the author describes a football match between the British and German soldiers. The **powerful verbs** have been taken out and weak verbs used instead. Change each of the weak verbs in bold to a **powerful verb**.

> The game **went** back and forth across No Man's Land. The goalpost **got** larger as greatcoats and tunics **were taken off** as the players got into the sport. Khaki and grey were together. Steam **came** from their backs and their faces **were covered** in smiles and clouds of breath in the clear frosty air.

79

Unit 5 Let slip the dogs of war / fiction

War Game

Activity / **5.1**

WRITING

Story endings

> Deciding on how your story will end is an important part of planning. Not every story should end 'happily-ever-after'. *War Game* has a **cliff-hanger** ending where there are questions unanswered:
> - Has Will died?
> - Is he still alive but unconscious?
> - Will he get out of the shell hole?
> - What has happened to his friends?

Language features

What is the reader expecting?

- **The football match**
  The British and German troops play football with each other. The war seems to be forgotten. Perhaps there will be a happy ending?
- **The officers**
  The officers do not like them playing football with the 'enemy'. They are ordered back to the trenches. Perhaps they will have to go on fighting and there will not be a happy ending?
- **The German attack**
  The Germans attack but are forced back by '*rapid and deadly fire from the British*'. There is still a chance for a happy ending if the British prove too strong for the Germans.
- **Over the parapet**
  The British soldiers 'go over the top' and we read that '*The whole line went down ... and Will found himself in a shell hole staring at the sky. Then everything went black.*' The reader feels hopeless. Is Will dead? Are any of his friends still alive?

The cliff-hanger ending

We are left wondering if Will is alive. If he is alive will he be rescued? Will he be captured? Will he see any of his friends again?

Writing assignment

Write a short story with a cliff-hanger ending. You should:
- have no more than three characters
- make the reader unsure of how your story will end as some things go right and some things go wrong
- think about the questions your ending will leave unanswered.

You can use one of the titles below or an idea of your own:

| It Wouldn't Have Happened If... | The Accident | All in a Day's Work |

Unit 5 Let slip the dogs of war / fiction

The scream cut through the air...

This short story is told from the point of view of the Mission Commander. Early on in the story he speaks to his men before they are to go into battle:

'You are part of the finest, best-equipped and most scientific army that the world has ever seen. We were not sent here to fight, but we brought weapons with us because the Government knew that these people who use the word 'peace' so often, who profess to bring brotherhood and prosperity to the whole world, have nothing but hatred and envy in their hearts.'

The men are sent off to break camp and prepare to march. The Mission Commander is talking to his second in command when...

The scream cut through the air like a spurt of blood. Three of our men, their uniforms mud-splattered and torn, were running as fast as Olympic champions. Behind them there was a fourth. He was holding his side as he ran, leaving a trail of red spots, each one bigger than the last.

Mission Control: Hannibal One

Extract / **5.2**

The whole unit broke <u>formation</u> as the three men of the advance party ran past them without even a glance at their <u>comrades</u>. The fourth man was level with me now, and I stepped out to stand in his path. He stopped. His eyes were huge and full of tears. 'You said they were men!' he accused. 'You said we'd be fighting *men*!' His voice was shrill to the point of <u>hysteria</u>. His helmet was <u>askew</u>, but the spider of blood on his jaw told me he was the boy I'd spoken with. I grabbed his arm but he broke away from me with a surprising force. I looked down and found that my tunic was smeared with fresh shiny blood from the youngster's wounds. I watched him as he followed the others down a steep incline, dodging between the rocky outcrops. 'Come back!' I shouted. The wind snatched my voice away. I cupped my hands round my mouth, 'Come back at once! I'll have you executed!'

It was no use. The rest of them had sniffed the scent of panic and were scrambling down the hillside too. Only a few of the hardiest old campaigners remained in the roadway looking the way the four men had come. For a moment I had hope, but then they saw the sight that the others had seen and they too gibbered with fear.

'Don't be afraid,' I said, 'don't be afraid. I've seen them before. They are large, but they are controlled by men no better than us.'

Two of my senior sergeants then prostrated themselves on the roadway, screaming a mixture of prayers and oaths that betrayed a mankind for whom witchcraft lay just under the skin of science.

Other soldiers were ripping their hands and legs on the rocks and stony ledges below me as they half-ran and half-fell towards the sheltered basin in which we had camped the previous night, 'Alive!' my soldiers were shouting. 'They are alive! They are alive!'

They would not escape. There was no escape from here. Already some of the men who had fallen were not able to regain their feet. A thousand feet below me were men who could have got there only by throwing themselves bodily from the narrow crevasse. Wearily, I turned back to where my second-in-command was standing. He'd not moved.

'Who could have believed it?' I asked, as I stood there with the bald officer: just two of us between the invaders and the rich, lush land of Italy. 'Who could have believed that Hannibal would bring elephants over the Alps?'

Len Deighton

COMPREHENSION

A Write 'true' or 'false' for each of these statements.

1. The Mission Commander speaks to the men about why they are here.
2. The soldiers have been sent to fight.
3. The fourth soldier was wounded.
4. All of the soldiers ran away.
5. Hannibal had brought elephants over the Alps.

Unit 5 Let slip the dogs of war / fiction

B 1 Why do you think the Mission Commander praises his army at the beginning?

2 What simile is used to describe the *scream*?

3 The fourth man shouts, *'You said we'd be fighting men!'* At this point in the story, what did you think he had seen?

4 Why do you think *'a few of the hardiest old campaigners'* didn't run away?

5 How do you know that the men had never seen elephants before?

C 1 After the Commander's speech, did you think that the army would be successful or not? Why?

2 In what way was the ending of the story a surprise?

VOCABULARY

Use a dictionary and the context of the passage to explain the meaning of these words. They are underlined in the passage. The first one is done for you.

1 prosperity = wealth   2 spurt   3 formation

4 comrades   5 hysteria   6 askew

SPELLING

> The suffixes **ous** and **ious** can be confusing! Sometimes you can hear the 'i'.
>
> eg ser-**i**-ous = ser**ious**   victor-**i**-ous = victor**ious**
>
> Sometimes you can't hear the 'i' and it sounds like 'ous'.
>
> eg cons**cious**   fero**cious**

A Finish the answers to the clues by adding **ous** or **ious**. The first one is done for you.

1 wonderful = marvellous   2 tasty = delic _____

3 solemn = ser _____   4 having a religion = relig _____

5 being a winner = victor _____   6 giving freely = gener _____

> To add **ous** or **ious** to words ending in 'our', leave out the 'u' in the root word.
>
> eg vigour + **ous** = vigorous

B Add **ous** or **ious** to these root words.

1 vapour   2 humour   3 labour   4 glamour

Mission Control: Hannibal One

Activity / **5.2**

GRAMMAR AND PUNCTUATION

Direct speech

> We use speech marks ' ' at the beginning and end of what a character actually says.
>
> eg   'Come back at once!'   — speech mark at the end
> speech mark   spoken words   punctuation before
> at the beginning   speech mark

In print, single inverted commas are generally used for all quotations (direct or indirect); in handwriting, double inverted commas are often used to enclose direct speech.

A Copy and punctuate these **direct speech** sentences. The first one is done for you.

1 You will do your duty ordered the Commander.
   'You will do your duty,' ordered the Commander.

2 Run screamed the wounded soldier.

3 Stand and fight bellowed the Commander.

4 Alive my soldiers were shouting.

5 What are they asked the second-in-command.

6 Who would have believed it he said.

HINT
Look for the spoken words.

> When a different person speaks we begin a new paragraph.
>
> eg   'What have you seen?' asked the soldier as he stared fearfully across the mountains.
>   'They're huge! They're alive!' screamed the wounded man.

B Copy the conversation below. Add the correct punctuation marks. Begin a new line when a different character speaks.

> What sort of weapons do you think they will bring with them asked Marcus. I don't know replied Gaius. Have you ever seen Hannibal's army before asked Marcus. I've heard about it but I've never seen it said Gaius.

Unit 5 Let slip the dogs of war /fiction

Mission Control: Hannibal One

Activity / **5.2**

WRITING

Story endings

> Story writers like to keep their readers guessing about the **ending**. Even if everything turns out well in the end, a writer does not want you to guess this from the very beginning!
>
> In this story, the writer makes you think you are reading about a modern army. At the very end we realise that it is about Hannibal's battle against the Romans in 216 BC!

Language features

Vocabulary choices

The writer uses words which lead readers to think they are reading a modern war story.

    eg   *'Mission Control'*   *'comrades'*   *'scientific'*

We feel that this is a modern army on a peace-keeping mission.

He also uses words that will not 'give the game away'.

    eg   *'uniforms'*   *'unit'*   *'advance party'*   *'helmet'*

All these words could be used in almost any war story.

Clues

We think we are reading a modern war story but the writer gives us clues which puzzle us.

    eg The wounded soldier shouts, *'You said we'd be fighting **men**!'*

Has he seen tanks or planes carrying bombs?

The surprise ending

The writer leaves us guessing until the very end when we read:

> *'Who could have believed it?...Who could have believed that Hannibal would bring elephants over the Alps?'*

Writing assignment

Write a short story with a surprise ending. You should:

- have no more than three characters
- disguise what is really going on in your story
- surprise the reader at the very end.

You can use one of the titles below or an idea of your own:

    My First Day   A Tricky Situation   Discovery!

Unit 5 Let slip the dogs of war / fiction

And they just kept coming...

Meteorites have landed on Earth bringing with them strange plants which suck people's blood and kill them. Jack Meredith and Sally Lewis are the scientists who have to beat the invaders. So far, they have failed...

Thousands of seeds had blown far and wide, all around the world.

The seeds were worse than the plants. If they landed on a person or animal, they started sending a root down into the skin...

Jack was sitting in his garden, reading the papers. Reports of deaths were coming in from all over the world. Some people had been sprayed with <u>pollen</u>, then sucked dry while they lay helplessly on the ground. Others had been victims of the seeds.

Next door, his neighbour, Mr Parry, was busy working. Jack went over to talk to him.

'I've never seen your roses look better, Mr Parry.'

'That's because there's no greenfly around this year,' said the old gardener. 'They've all disappeared.'

Jack was surprised at this. Greenfly were always a problem.

'Why do you think that is?'

'That's easy!' said Mr Parry. 'You don't eat bread and water when you can get steak, do you! The greenfly have found something <u>tastier</u> to eat!'

He pointed to the corner of his garden. One of the yellow plants was growing there.

'Mr Parry! That's a very dangerous plant!'

'It doesn't look dangerous to me. And it helps my roses!'

Jack looked closely. The yellow plant was covered in greenfly. They were sucking the juice out of the leaves. It was nearly dead already!

Jack rushed indoors to the telephone. Maybe the problem was solved.

Space Weed

Extract / 5.3

Later that day, Jack rang Sally at her home. It had been a bad day for Jack.

'No one in the government will listen!' he said. They say that I only make things worse!'

'Forget the government,' said Sally. 'You've got a computer. Tell the world! Put what you have found on the Internet!'

Within minutes, the message was on the World Wide Web. 'Common greenfly will kill the plants. If you do not have them in your country, send for them. Release them near the plants. They will do the rest.'

Britain had plenty of greenfly. The strange plants were being sucked to death. The government was delighted. Jack's mistakes were soon forgiven.

One morning, Jack was sitting in the garden again. Mr Parry did not seem to be a happy man today.

'Look at my garden! Ruined!'

The roses were all dead. Jack looked closely at them. Greenfly! But he had never seen greenfly that big before!

They were huge, at least five times as big as normal. They were moving off the roses, looking for something else to eat.

Jack could guess what had happened. The greenfly had drunk the juices of the plants. The plant was full of strange chemicals. The greenfly had changed. They would breed, and maybe destroy all plant life on Earth! He hadn't been able to kill the plants with poison. He guessed that the greenfly couldn't be killed that way either.

He had told the world to release greenfly. It was all his fault – again!

He didn't think things could get much worse.

There were no living plants left in the gardens. They had all been sucked dry by the greenfly. It was then he felt a sharp pain on his hand. Then another one on his face.

The greenfly had eaten all the plants. Now they were looking for blood.

And they just kept coming.

David Orme

COMPREHENSION

A Choose the best answer for each question.

1. Jack went to talk to Mr Parry who was:
   a reading a newspaper   b working in the garden
   c lying helplessly on the ground.

2. The roses looked good because:
   a they had been sprayed with pollen   b they were fed on bread and water
   c there were no greenfly around.

3. Sally told Jack to tell the world about the greenfly by:
   a using the computer   b using the telephone   c writing letters.

4. Britain had plenty of:
   a roses   b steak   c greenfly.

5. Jack had never seen greenfly:
   a so yellow   b so huge   c so strange.

Unit 5 Let slip the dogs of war / fiction

B 1 How did the plants kill people?

2 What do you think Mr Parry is saying about the dangerous plants when he says:
'You don't eat bread and water when you can get steak'?

3 When Jack saw the greenfly killing the dangerous plant why did he think:
'Maybe the problem was solved'?

4 Why did Jack think that poison would not kill the greenfly?

5 When the greenfly had killed all the plant life, what do you think they would eat next?

C Were you expecting the ending, or were you surprised?
Explain your reasons.

VOCABULARY

Use a dictionary and the context of the story to explain the meanings of these words. They are underlined in the passage. The first one is done for you.

1 pollen = *yellow powder*   2 tastier   3 release

4 delighted   5 ruined   6 breed

SPELLING

> The strange plant was notice**able** in Mr Parry's garden.
> Greenfly were vis**ible** all over the plant.
>
> It is not easy to decide when to use **able** and when to use **ible**!
>
> - If the opposite of the word is made by adding the prefix **un**, then it is probably an **able** word.
>
>   eg **un** + notice**able** = *un*notice*able*
>
> - If the opposite of the word is made by adding the prefix **in**, then it is probably an **ible** word.
>
>   eg **in** + cred**ible** = *in*cred*ible*

A Copy and complete the words below with **able** or **ible**.
The first one is done for you.

1 unsuit _____ = *unsuitable*   2 invis _____

3 insens _____   4 unus _____

5 invalu _____   6 unlov _____

7 unreason _____   8 unbeliev _____

> **HINT**
>
> Many more words end in 'able' than 'ible'.

B Use one **able** and one **ible** word you have made in sentences of your own.

Space Weed

Activity / 5.3

GRAMMAR AND PUNCTUATION

Conditional sentences

> A **conditional sentence** is where one action depends upon another. eg
>
> *The seeds sent roots into the skin if they landed on a person.*
>   main clause   conditional clause
>
> The sentence is made up of:
> - a main clause
> - a conditional clause – usually beginning with **if**.

A Copy and complete these **conditional sentences**.

1. Roses will grow really well if _____.
2. The problem would be solved if _____.
3. Jack could tell the world about the greenfly if _____.
4. The greenfly would only eat the roses if _____.
5. All plant life would be destroyed if _____.

> If the **conditional clause** comes first in the sentence, it is separated from the main clause by a comma. eg
>
> *If you do not have greenfly in your country , send for them.*
>   conditional clause   comma main clause

B Add a main clause to each of these conditional clauses to complete each sentence.

1. If Jack was to save the world _____.
2. If there is life on other planets _____.
3. If strange plants landed on Earth _____.
4. If I found a strange plant in my garden _____.
5. If roses are covered in greenfly _____.

HINT

Remember the comma.

Unit 5 **Let slip the dogs of war** / fiction

Space Weed

Activity / **5.3**

WRITING

Story endings

> Writers do not want you to guess the **ending** of a story but they will give you *clues* as to how it might turn out.
>
> In *Space Weed* we know that the plants are dangerous and that Jack is trying to do all he can to get rid of them. The greenfly seem to be the answer – but are they?

Language features

Building tension

The writer wants us to know how dangerous the situation is. We are told that:

- *'Thousands of seeds had blown far and wide, all around the world.'*
- People were *'sucked dry while they lay helplessly on the ground'*.

The situation is very tense. What can Jack do?

Changing the mood

After the first two paragraphs, we feel that everything is hopeless but then the writer changes the mood. Greenfly can kill the plants! Jack puts this hopeful message on the web:

> *'Common greenfly will kill the plants. If you do not have them in your country, send for them. Release them near the plants. They will do the rest.'*

Suddenly there is hope! The plants can be killed! Everyone will be safe!

The surprise ending!

We think Jack has solved the problem but we are in for a nasty surprise! The greenfly have eaten the plants but they have become just as dangerous:

> *'The greenfly had drunk the juices of the plants. The plant was full of strange chemicals. The greenfly had changed.'*

So now the plants are not the problem but the greenfly are. With no plants left to eat, the greenfly start to eat people!

Writing assignment

Write a short story where the reader is given clues as to how it might end.

- If your story is going to end happily, make sure there is a time when things go wrong.
- If your story is going to end unhappily, make sure there is a time when things look hopeful.

You can use one of the titles below or an idea of your own:

The Visitor   A Day Out   An Unusual Journey

Unit 6 All the world's a stage / drama

Scene: A living room...

MOTHER	Stephen? Come on, it's dinner time!
STEPHEN	What are we eating?
LINDA	Pork!
MOTHER	Pork chops.
STEPHEN	I don't want any.
MOTHER	What do you mean?
LINDA	It's your favourite, you're always asking for it.
STEPHEN	I just don't want any. I'd like an egg. Two eggs. I'll do them myself.
MOTHER	No you won't young man. Those are for breakfast. If you go on like this I'll be cross. Dad'll be home soon and I want the rest of you out of the way. He's had a long day and he wants to have his dinner in peace.
LINDA	(*sitting down*) Well, I'm not waiting.
MOTHER	(*sitting down too*) You can join us or not as you please but leave the eggs alone.
STEPHEN	(*still not sitting down*) I'm a <u>vegetarian</u>.
MOTHER	What?
STEPHEN	A vegetarian.
LINDA	Hark at him, he must have gone <u>religious</u>.
STEPHEN	No I haven't. I just don't eat meat.
MOTHER	Stephen, for heaven's sake, why?
STEPHEN	It's wrong.
LINDA	But you do eat meat. You've eaten it every day for fourteen years.
STEPHEN	And now I've stopped.
MOTHER	What, just like that?
STEPHEN	Yes. I think it's <u>immoral</u>.

Animal Rights

Extract / 6.1

MOTHER   Stephen, if this is your idea of a joke it's gone far enough. Your chops will go cold with all this fooling about.

STEPHEN   But I'm serious. I mean what I say.

LINDA   Don't worry Mum, it's only a phase. It'll be something else next week. You know what he's like.

STEPHEN   (*shouting*) I mean what I say!

MOTHER   Well, after all we've done for you. Here's your father, look, for the last time… (*Stephen shakes his head*)

MOTHER   (*furious*) I didn't buy this expensive food for you to waste it!

FATHER   (*coming in*) Hey, what's going on? What's he been doing, what have you done, my lad?

STEPHEN   Nothing Dad.

LINDA   Dad, he's had a religious conversion!

MOTHER   He says he's a vegetarian. He won't eat meat.

FATHER   (*amused*) Well, that's his funeral, isn't it? He'll soon get hungry. Anyway, I'm hungry, and whatever you've made it smells good.

MOTHER   Sit down darling, I'll dish it up.

FATHER   Thanks, mm, very good (*taking a big forkful*). Excellent. (*Stephen is standing stubbornly with his arms folded*) Who put you up to this? You're no vegetarian, you're a carnivore through and through. Whose idea was it?

STEPHEN   My idea. I've been thinking.

LINDA   Hark at him! What next?

STEPHEN   Animals have as much right to live as we do.

FATHER   Rights? What do you know about rights? In this life you get what you get. This sheep probably got more out of life than you do.

STEPHEN   We killed it. Anyway it's not a sheep, it's a pig.

LINDA   Was a pig. Dirty things…

STEPHEN   Pigs are famous for being affectionate.

LINDA   Mum, I know what it is! It's that film about the pig he saw last week, the pig that got stolen and everybody wanted to eat! It sounded stupid to me!

Michael Church and Betty Tadman

COMPREHENSION

A   Copy these sentences. Fill in the missing words.

1. The family are having __ __ __ __ for dinner.
2. Stephen is __ __ __ __ __ __ __ __ years old.
3. Stephen says he is a __ __ __ __ __ __ __ __ __ __ and will not eat meat.
4. He says that __ __ __ __ __ __ __ have as much right to live as humans.
5. Linda says that pigs are __ __ __ __ __ things.

Unit 6 All the world's a stage / drama

B 1 What does Stephen's mother think of him being a vegetarian?
  2 What does Linda think of Stephen being a vegetarian?
  3 What does Stephen's father mean when he says:
    'You're a carnivore through and through'?
  4 How do you know that Stephen's father thinks someone has put the idea into his son's head?
  5 Where does Linda think he got the idea from?

C Stephen says, 'Animals have as much right to live as we do.'
   What do you think?

VOCABULARY

Use a dictionary and the context of the play to find the meanings of these words. They are underlined in the script. The first one is done for you.

1 vegetarian = *someone who does not eat meat*

2 religious   3 immoral   4 phase

5 conversion   6 carnivore

SPELLING

> Adding the suffix **ful** to a noun makes it into an adjective.
>   eg peace + **ful** = *peaceful*
>   *peaceful* means full of peace

A Add the suffix **ful** to each of these words. The first one is done for you.

1 force = *forceful*   2 care   3 hope

4 dread   5 sorrow   6 thought

HINT

Remember! There is only one l in the suffix 'ful'.

> If a noun ends in **y**, we usually change the y to i before adding a suffix.
>   eg beau**y** + **ful** = *beautiful*

B Add the suffix **ful** to each of these words. The first one is done for you.

1 fancy = *fanciful*   2 plenty   3 mercy

4 duty   5 bounty

Animal Rights

Activity / **6.1**

GRAMMAR AND PUNCTUATION

Active and passive verbs

> In a sentence:
> - the subject does the action
> - the verb is the action
> - the object has the action done to it.
>   eg *Father ate the pork*.
>   subject verb object
>
> This pattern: subject + verb + object = **active voice**

A Copy the sentences. Underline:
- the subject in <u>red</u>
- the verb in <u>blue</u>
- the object in <u>green</u>.

The first one is done for you.

1 <u>Mother</u> <u>cooked</u> <u>the dinner</u>.
2 Stephen wanted eggs.
3 Father ate the chops.
4 They killed the pig.
5 Linda mocked Stephen.
6 Stephen didn't eat the meat.

> Some sentences have a different pattern.
>   eg *The pork was eaten by Father*.
>   object   verb   subject
>
> This pattern: object + verb + subject = **passive voice**

B Copy the sentences. Underline:
- the object in <u>green</u>
- the verb in <u>blue</u>
- the subject in <u>red</u>.

The first one is done for you.

1 <u>The dinner</u> <u>was cooked</u> by <u>Mother</u>.
2 The eggs were wanted by Stephen.
3 The chops were eaten by Father.
4 The pig was killed by them.
5 Stephen was mocked by Linda.
6 The meat was not eaten by Stephen.

Unit 6 All the world's a stage / drama

98

Animal Rights

Activity / **6.1**

WRITING

Playscripts

> A **playscript** is set out in the following way:
> - The names of the characters who are speaking are on the left. You can use capital letters or bold.
>   eg 'LINDA'
> - What the characters say, ie the dialogue, is written next to each name.
>   eg 'LINDA   Pork!'
> - Stage directions which tell a character how to speak or move are written in italics and/or put in brackets.
>   eg '(*sitting down*)'

Language features

Setting the scene

The playwright tells you where the action is taking place: ie '*Scene: A living room*'

Dialogue

Playwrights try to write in the way people speak. They use:
- pauses   eg '*Thanks, mm, very good. (taking a big forkful) Excellent.*'
- incomplete sentences eg '*Was a pig. Dirty things...*'
- one-word sentences   eg '*Pork!*'

Stage directions

These help actors and actresses to know:
- how to say a line   eg '(*amused*) Well, that's his funeral, isn't it?'
- what action to make eg '(*Stephen shakes his head.*)'

Writing assignment

Write the next scene of *Animal Rights*. You need to plan:

- where the scene takes place: Is it in the living-room or somewhere else?
- the time of the scene: Is it the same day, the next day or later?
- the characters in the scene: Will there be a new character?
- what will be discussed among the   Does anyone think he is right?
  characters about Stephen's decision: Does Stephen change his mind?

Set your playscript out using:
- one colour for the characters' names
- a different colour for the dialogue
- a third colour for the stage directions.

Unit 6 All the world's a stage / drama

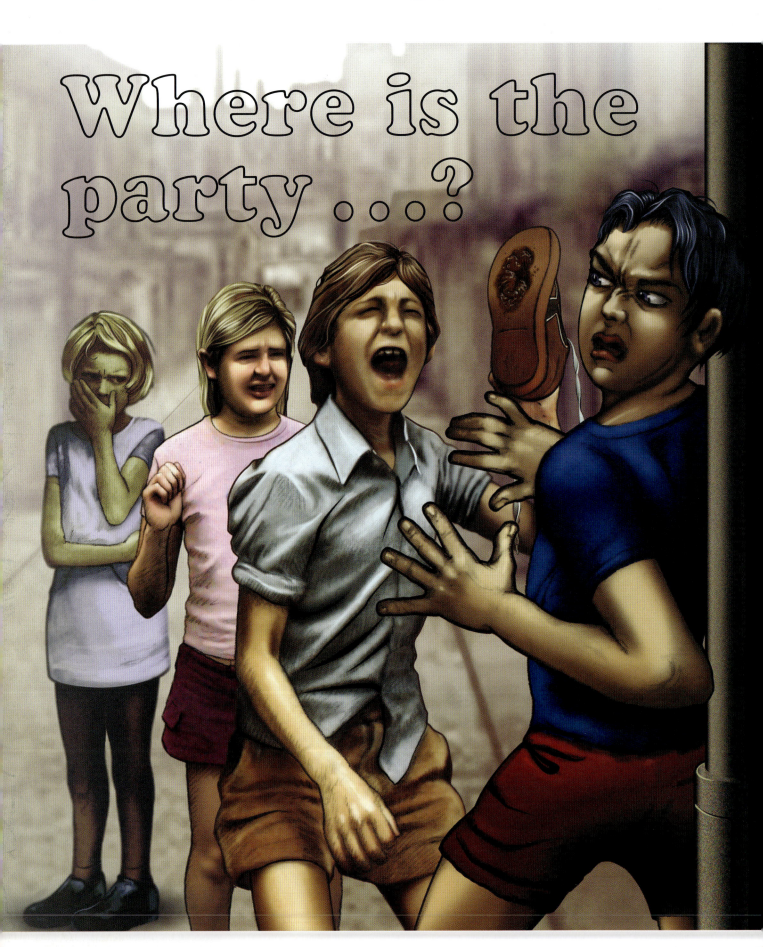

Kidsplay

Extract / **6.2**

Scene: A back alley (a 'ten-foot') in a town. Penny and Val appear.

VAL   Where is the party, though?
PENNY   I don't know ... it's somewhere round here. What's Willie doing? (*Willie enters, trailing his foot.*)
WILLIE   Orr, I've got <u>dog-cack</u> on me shoe!
PENNY   Oh, Willie! Wipe it off then!
WILLIE   I can't!
PENNY   Well, take your shoe off, then! (*Willie removes his shoe. They all look at it and go 'Yeeeurgh!' Willie cannot resist having a close-up sniff.*)
WILLIE   Poooh! It stinks! Smell it!
PENNY   I can already smell it from here!
WILLIE   (*Thrusting the shoe at Penny*) Smell it close! Go on!
PENNY   Nooo-o! Take it away!
WILLIE   I dare you to smell it!
PENNY   No, I'm not going to smell it!
WILLIE   Well ... Touch it then! Go on! You daren't.
VAL   No! Don't! (*Penny decides to touch it.*)
PENNY   Yeeurgh! Err, it's all <u>yacky</u> and squidgy!
VAL   Orr, Penny! Err ... it's horrible!
PENNY   What shall I do with it?
WILLIE   Get Valerie to lick it off!!
VAL   No! Take it away!
PENNY   <u>Orr</u>, alright, I'll wipe it on this lamp-post,
WILLIE   <u>Yeeach</u>! I hate ten-foots – they're horrible!
PENNY   No, they're not ... they're good – I wish we had one!
WILLIE   I don't! They're dirty and smelly and common ... (*Martin appears suddenly through his gate and crosses straight to Willie.*)
MARTIN   I'm <u>gonna</u> smack you!
WILLIE   (*Leaping back in alarm*) What for?
PENNY   (*Standing in front of Willie*) No, you're not!
MARTIN   Yeah, I am. I'm gonna smack you!
WILLIE   No you're not, then ... '<u>cos</u> I'll rub dog-cacca up your nose!
PENNY   Yeah! Go on, Willie! (*Willie thrusts the shoe at Martin's face. Martin backs off, squirming. Willie presses forward the attack.*)
WILLIE   (*Turning back*) He's running away, Penny! He's running. (*Martin advances.*)
WILLIE   He's coming back. Penny! He's coming back!!

John Lee

COMPREHENSION

A Write 'true' or 'false' for each of these statements.

1. Val and Penny are looking for the party.
2. Penny has trodden in dog-muck.
3. Penny says she will wipe the shoe on the lamp-post.
4. Willie is going to smack Martin.
5. Martin runs away.

Unit 6 All the world's a stage / drama

B Look closely at what the characters say and do. What impression do you get of:

a Penny b Val
c Willie d Martin?

C Do you think the conversation between the children is realistic or not? Explain your answer.

VOCABULARY

Use the context of the playscript to work out what these slang expressions mean. They are underlined in the script. The first one is done for you.

1 dog-cack = *dog muck*   2 yacky   3 Orr
4 Yeeach   5 gonna   6 'cos

SPELLING

A **contraction** is where two words are joined and the missing letters are replaced with an apostrophe.
  eg what **is** = *what's*
      you **ha**ve = *you've*

A Write these contractions as two words. The first one is done for you.

1 it's = *it is*   2 I've   3 I'm
4 they're   5 he's   6 that's

Not as **n't** is used in many contractions.
  eg would **not** = *wouldn't*
      did **not** = *didn't*

B Write the contractions of these phrases. The first one is done for you.

1 dare not = *daren't*   2 could not   3 should not
4 might not   5 cannot   6 do not

C What is the contraction here:

1 shall not   2 will not

HINT
Put the ' where the letters would have been.

Kidsplay   Activity / **6.2**

GRAMMAR AND PUNCTUATION

Punctuating a playscript

> When we speak we do not always use complete sentences. We pause, repeat ourselves, shout, whisper, umm and er!
>
> In *Kidsplay* the writer has used all these things to make the speech seem natural. **Punctuation** is useful for this:
>
> - exclamation marks (!), used to show the tone of voice
>   eg *WILLIE 'Poooh! It stinks! (disgusted)'*
> - dots (...), used to show pauses
>   eg '*VAL Err... it's horrible.*'
> - dashes (–), also used to show pauses. What comes after a dash is usually emphasised.
>   eg '*PENNY No, they're not... they're good – I wish we had one!*'

Copy the lines of dialogue in the box below. Use an exclamation mark, dots or a dash where there are brackets.

> TOM   Is this the right shop?
> FRED   I don't know ( ) I think so.
> TOM   You must remember where you bought the trainers ( )
> FRED   Well, I thought ( ) wait a minute ( )
> TOM   You've remembered ( )
> FRED   Yes ( ) this is the shop ( )
> TOM   Great ( ) I thought we'd be wandering about all day ( )
> FRED   Just a minute ( ) No ( ) It's closed down ( )

Unit 6 All the world's a stage / drama

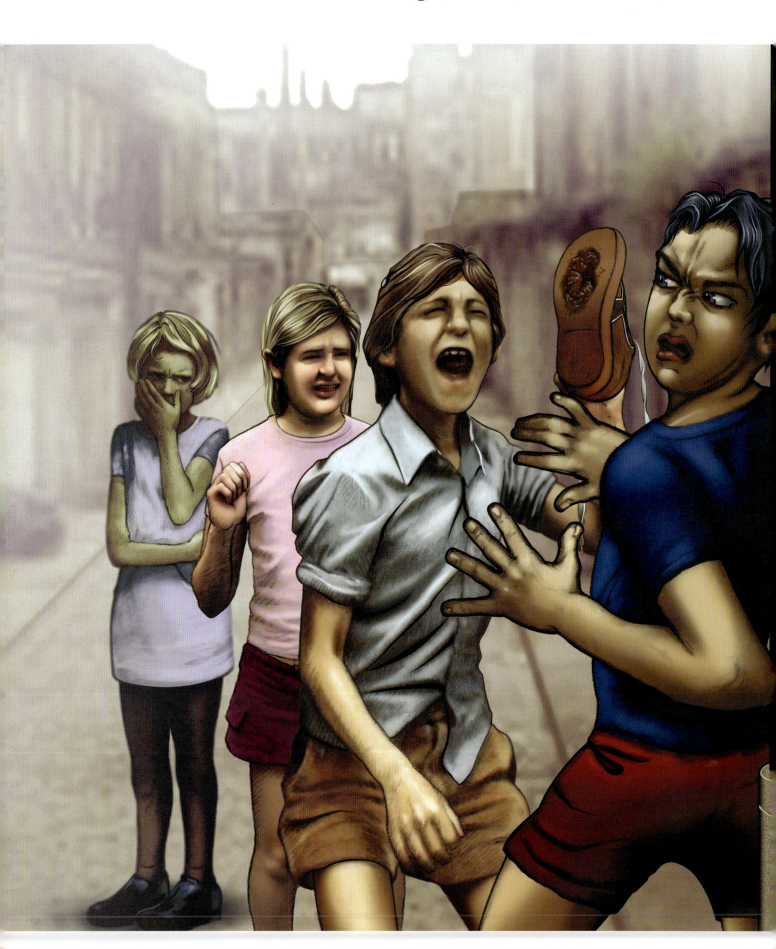

104

WRITING

Dramatic dialogue

> Writing **dialogue** which sounds like people talking isn't easy! Playwrights have to decide what kind of people the characters are. The audience gets to know the characters by what they say and do.

Language features

Dramatic dialogue

A playwright has to think about how characters would speak:
- Do they have an accent?
- Do they use slang?
- What kind of vocabulary would they use?
- How would they speak in certain situations?

Punctuation

Once a playwright has decided how the characters would speak, he has to use punctuation to make it sound natural:
- exclamation marks show tone of voice and emphasis
- dots create dramatic pauses
- dashes create pauses and show that what is to follow is important.

Writing assignment

Write a conversation between two characters in a scene of your choice. Here are some suggestions.

scene

| a room in a house | a street | in a wood | in space |

characters

| calm and reasonable | timid, cries easily | a bully |
| a loner, very quiet | likeable, sensible | dishonest |

In the conversation the two characters are having a disagreement. Set out your conversation as a playscript. Remember:
- set the scene
- characters' names on the left
- dialogue on the right – remember the punctuation
- stage directions in brackets.

Unit 6 All the world's a stage / drama

Hey, Blousey...

The action takes place in New York in 1929. It is the era of gangsters and 'prohibition' when the buying and selling of alcohol in public places was banned. The gangsters ran the illegal trade in alcohol in secret clubs known as 'speakeasies'. Blousey works in one of these clubs. Bugsy Malone is not totally honest but is not truly a gangster.

The lights come up on Bugsy in the phone booth at the side of the stage.

BLOUSEY Hello.
BUGSY Hey Blousey, it's Bugsy.
BLOUSEY Where are you?
BUGSY Oh around. Listen. I can't talk to you now but I've just made two hundred <u>bucks</u>.
BLOUSEY You mean you printed it yourself?
BUGSY No I earned it, swear to God. *(Crosses himself)*
BLOUSEY Doing what?
BUGSY Oh this and that.
BLOUSEY Who for?
BUGSY Fat Sam.
BLOUSEY Fat Sam gave you 200 dollars?
BUGSY And the loan of his <u>sedan</u> for the afternoon.
BLOUSEY I don't believe you. You're putting me on.
BUGSY Look, if you get yourself outside the Grand Slam in ten minutes, look for the <u>snazzy</u> sedan with the good-looking driver and you'll find he has a very close <u>resemblance</u> to yours truly...O.K.?
BLOUSEY O.K. But you'd better not be putting me on, Buster.
BUGSY Cross my heart it's on the level. So long. *(The light goes down on Bugsy and Blousey puts on her hat and coat and exits... Lights up on side of the stage where Blousey is sitting on a swing – Bugsy enters with two hot dogs.)*

Bugsy Malone

Extract / 6.3

BUGSY   Mustard with onions, Ketchup without.

BLOUSEY   Ketchup without. Do you really have 200 dollars?

BUGSY   Nope.

BLOUSEY   Oh yeah, you lied.

BUGSY   No, I've got 198 dollars and ten cents – I just bought two hot dogs.

BLOUSEY   You didn't do anything <u>crooked</u>, did you?

BUGSY   Of course not. I got it for driving and for helping Mr Sam out of a little <u>predicament</u>. Oh, I nearly forgot. (*He hands a parcel to her. A big shoe-box tied with a ribbon.*)

BLOUSEY   What's this, a fingerbowl?

BUGSY   No, a present wisie!

BLOUSEY   For me?

BUGSY   (*He looks around him*) Well I didn't buy it for the audience…

BLOUSEY   Oh Bugsy, it's wonderful. Fantastic. What is it? (*She looks through the wrong end of an old photo viewer.*)

BUGSY   A viewer, dummy. (*He turns it round the correct way*) Look, you turn the handle. All the Hollywood stars.

BLOUSEY   Oh, if only I could get to Hollywood.

BUGSY   You can.

BLOUSEY   Oh sure, I've heard that one, wise guy … in the front row of the Roxy on East 38th Street

BUGSY   No, really get to Hollywood. (*She beckons back with her thumb.*) You want me to leave?

BLOUSEY   No, push me, dummy, and keep talking

BUGSY   I've got 198 dollars and 10 cents left, right? What does that buy?

BLOUSEY   Er … (*Counting on her fingers*) 440 hot dogs.

BUGSY   No, two tickets, stupid.

BLOUSEY   Two tickets?

BUGSY   On the Super Chief.

BLOUSEY   Super Chief?

BUGSY   The train, dummy! To Hollywood. Think about it.

Alan Parker

COMPREHENSION

A Choose the best answer for each question.

1. Bugsy said he had:
   a earned 200 dollars   b stolen 200 dollars   c won 200 dollars.

2. Bugsy is going to pick Blousey up:
   a on a bike   b in a taxi   c in a car.

3. The two hot dogs cost:
   a more than 2 dollars   b less than 2 dollars   c 200 dollars.

4. Bugsy buys Blousey:
   a a fingerbowl   b a sedan   c a viewer.

5. Bugsy is going to buy two tickets to:
   a Hollywood   b East 38th Street   c the Roxy.

Unit 6 All the world's a stage / drama

B 1 What was Blousey suggesting when she asked if Bugsy had *'printed'* the 200 dollars?

2 How do you know that Blousey finds it difficult to trust Bugsy?

3 Do you think that what Bugsy did for Fat Sam was legal or illegal? Why?

4 What sort of person do you think Blousey is?

5 Blousey's dream is to get to Hollywood. What do you think she wants to do there?

C Imagine you were going to set the scene for Bugsy and Blousey in the park eating hot dogs. List the things you would need on the stage to make it look like a real park.

VOCABULARY

Use a dictionary and the context of the script to explain the meanings of these words. They are underlined in the script. The first one is done for you.

1 bucks = *dollars*
2 sedan
3 snazzy
4 resemblance
5 crooked
6 predicament

SPELLING

> Remember: **apostrophes** are used when we miss out letters.
> eg *'You did**n't** (did **no**t) do anything crooked, did you?'*
> Apostrophes are also used to show who owns something.
> eg *Bugsy**'s** hot dog* = the hot dog belonging to Bugsy

A Write each phrase in a shorter way using an **apostrophe**. The first one has been done for you.

1 the money belonging to Bugsy = *Bugsy's money*

2 the dress belonging to Blousey
3 the car belonging to Fat Sam
4 the present belonging to Blousey
5 the tickets belonging to Bugsy

> Bugsy**'s** hot dog: by adding **'s** to Bugsy we make it into a **possessive** noun. Bugsy **possesses** the hot dog.

B Is the **'s** word in each of these phrases a **contraction** or a **possessive noun**? The first one is done for you.

1 he's happy = *contraction: he is happy*
2 Bugsy's car
3 Blousey's worried
4 Sam's sedan

108

Bugsy Malone

Activity / **6.3**

GRAMMAR AND PUNCTUATION

Standard English

> When we write we need to use English as carefully and correctly as possible. We need to:
> - think carefully about the choice of words
> - check spelling
> - use correct punctuation
> - write in sentences.
>
> This is called **Standard English**.
>
> When we speak, we use English more informally. Playscripts are written as if people are speaking. In *Bugsy Malone*, the playwright has written in **non-Standard English** to:
> - imitate the gangster films of the 1940 and 1950s
> - suggest an American setting
> - make the characters fast-thinking and street-wise.
>
> | eg | Standard English | Non-Standard English |
> |---|---|---|
> | | *yes* | *yeah* |
> | | *honestly* | *cross my heart* |

Change the phrases and sentences below into Standard English.

1. You're putting me on.
2. ...it's on the level
3. O.K.
4. So long.
5. Nope.
6. Yeah.
7. You didn't do anything crooked, did you?
8. wisie
9. wise guy
10. dummy

Unit 6 All the world's a stage / drama

Bugsy Malone

Activity / **6.3**

WRITING

Storyboarding a play scene

A **storyboard** is a series of pictures which show what should happen in a scene. A storyboard looks like a comic strip. Each picture is called a frame.

Each frame in the storyboard shows:
- the type of camera shot   eg   distant camera shot
- the angle of the camera   eg   from above
- the movement and direction of the camera   eg   zooms in
- the timing of the camera shot   eg   10 seconds
- the dialogue spoken   eg   Where are you?
- the special effects   eg   sound of trains

Language features

Below is an example of one frame of a storyboard. It helps the cameraman to know how to shoot the scene.

High camera angle

Medium camera shot

Zoom in slowly for 5 seconds

Special effects = pool of blood slowly seeping from under the body

Dialogue = Nobody squeals on Fat Sam!

Cut right to next camera shot →

Writing assignment

Make a storyboard for one of the following.

   Bugsy's telephone call to Blousey   Blousey and Bugsy in the park

Your storyboard should include:
- a picture of each part of the scene
- where you want the camera to shoot from
- any special effect, eg what can be seen? what can be heard?
- the dialogue spoken in each part of the scene.

Text © Wendy Wren 2005
Original illustrations © Nelson Thornes Ltd 2005

The right of Wendy Wren to be identified as author of this work has been asserted by her in accordance with the Copyright, Designs and Patents Act 1988.

All rights reserved. No part of this publication may be reproduced or transmitted in any form or by any means, electronic or mechanical, including photocopy, recording or any information storage and retrieval system, without permission in writing from the publisher or under licence from the Copyright Licensing Agency Limited, of 90 Tottenham Court Road, London W1T 4LP.

Any person who commits any unauthorised act in relation to this publication may be liable to criminal prosecution and civil claims for damages.

Published in 2005 by:
Nelson Thornes Ltd
Delta Place
27 Bath Road
CHELTENHAM
GL53 7TH
United Kingdom

05 06 07 08 09 / 10 9 8 7 6 5 4 3 2 1

A catalogue record for this book is available from the British Library

ISBN 0 7487 9340 2

Illustrations by Tom Barnfield, Jane Cope, Beverly Curl, Jim Eldridge, Angela Lumley, Zhenya Matysiak, Paul MaCaffery c/o Sylvie Poggio Artists Agency, Rod Waters

Designed by Viners Wood Associates

Printed and bound in China by Midas Printing International Ltd

The author and publishers wish to thank the following for permission to use copyright material:

Jim Alderson for material from his adapted version of Bram Stoker, *Dracula* (1973) pp. 16-8; Robert Clark, as Literary Executor for Leonard Clark, 'Owls'; Jonathan Clowes Ltd on behalf of the author for material from Len Deighton, *Declarations of War* (1971) pp. 106, 107-9, Copyright © 1971 Len Deighton; Chrysalis Children's Books, an imprint of Chrysalis Books Group Plc, for material from Michael Foreman, *War Game* (1997) pp. 76-9, 82-93, Copyright © 1997 Michael Foreman; Faber and Faber Ltd for material from William Golding, *Lord of the Flies* (1954) pp. 45-6; David Higham Associates on behalf of the author for Charles Causley, 'My Mother Saw a Dancing Bear' from *Collected Poems by Charles Causley*, Macmillan; John Lee for material from his *Kidsplay*, Act Now Plays, ed. Peter Rowlands, Cambridge University Press (1989) pp. 32-4;
The estate of Bill Naughton for material from his book, *The Goalkeeper's Revenge*; David Orme for material from his book, *Space Weed*, in the Zone 13 series; Alan Parker for material from his book, *Bugsy Malone*, National Film Trustee Company (1984); Pearson Education for material from George Layton, *The Fib and Other Stories*, Longman (1978) pp. 94-6; Michael Church and Betty Tadman, 'Animal Rights' from *Plays for Today*, Longman (1978) pp. 2-6;
The Random House Group Ltd for material from Jacqueline Wilson, *The Bed and Breakfast Star*, Doubleday (1994) pp. 174-6, 178; Franz Kafka, *Metamorphosis*, Secker & Warburg (1999) pp. 9, 10, 11; Terry Pratchett, *Johnny and the Dead*, Doubleday (1993) pp. 38-40; The Society of Authors as the Literary Representative of the Estate of the author for John Masefield, 'Reynard the Fox';

Every effort has been made to trace the copyright holders but if any have been inadvertently overlooked the publishers will be pleased to make the necessary arrangement at the first opportunity.